I0006866

About the Author

Ken Jaskulski purchased his first 286 computer in the early 80's and still works with computers daily. Ken owns Second Source Computers in Wilmington, DE. Second Source Computers was established in 1987 and to date has sold and serviced over 50,000 computers, tablets, phones and printers.

Second Source Computers has been voted "Readers Choice - Best Computer Store" by the local Wilmington newspaper readers when the award originated back in 2000 and as the place to get computers repaired by Delaware Today Magazine.

In 1995, Ken produced and wrote *Computers for Cowards*, a complete PC training and troubleshooting instructional video and manual. Ken wrote and produced *Computers for Cowards – Small Business Edition* in video format in 1997.

Ken self-published his first Computer Book in 2012 *Computer Secrets – Confessions of a Computer Tech*. Computer Secrets was carried in Barnes & Noble and sold on Amazon. *Computer Repair Smartiepants* is the first of a series of Smartiepants branded books written to give the reader inside information on specific topics in an easy to read and implement format.

Ken provides free computer tech tips on YouTube under pcwhispereronline and secondsourcecomputers.com and can be reached for computer help, consulting and deals on factory refurbished warranted computers at pcwhispereonline@gmail.com.

Today Ken still takes his dogs to work with him and repairs computers. In his spare time, Ken writes, blogs about computers and basketball and plays pickup basketball.

Author's Acknowledgements

LOUISE & ANNIE

For putting up with me for working on that stupid laptop in front of SVU reruns every night. Thank you for your sacrifices so that I could complete this project. Love yas.

CO-WORKERS

Thanks to all the people that helped me over the years – Modman, Dennis, RonE, Alex, and everyone else. Your love of computers and willingness to help customers is why we have outlasted the big box chain stores and continue to service our customers.

MY CUSTOMERS

To the loyal customers that have supported a local computer store all this time instead of spending their hard earned dollars elsewhere. Your continued support has allowed me to get up every morning, head to work wearing shorts with my dogs and sneak out every now and then to hit tennis balls with my daughter or play hoops. No regrets.

THANKS ALL

CHAPTERS

CHAPTERS

APPENDIX

INTRODUCTION

Hello and Welcome to Computer Repair Smartiepants. The following statements illustrate why this book is necessary:

- **OVER 85% OF ALL COMPUTER PROBLEMS ARE NOT COVERED UNDER WARRANTY.**
- **THE AVERAGE COMPUTER REPAIR USUALLY BEGINS AT $100.**
- **THE AVERAGE REPAIR DOWN TIME CAN BE UP TO TWO WEEKS.**

These estimates are based on 30 years' experience and over 50,000 computers serviced. A computer is can stop working for no reason, require multiple people to figure out the problem and no one will take responsibility for the repair. Name another device that has its own five stages of grief and recovery written about them.

HAS THIS HAPPENED TO YOU?

John just purchased a new Windows-based computer from a big box store. After one week of use, the computer won't get on the Internet. A popup message said that the system has a Ransomware virus and the virus can only be removed if the computer user calls the number on the screen and pay the company $250 to remove it.

John tried to run the anti-virus program on the computer but it would not remove the message or get the computer back online. John called his neighbor Ed, the local neighborhood computer guru. Ed tried but could not remove the popup. Ed suggested that John re-install Windows and start over.

The popups were so bad that John could not use a flash drive to back up the data. Assuming that John could re-install Windows, his documents would be lost that weren't backed up. John's son would also lose his documents, photos and ITunes that were downloaded to the system.

John called the store where he purchased the computer for help. After twenty minutes on-hold, John finally reached the store service department. The service rep told John that because he did not purchase the store extended warranty that John will have to call the computer manufacturer directly for assistance.

John's next step was to call the computer manufacturer. John's spoke to a level one support representative named Hassid. Hassid was very polite; however, spoke with an accent and was hard to understand.

Hassid read from a support script. After thirty minutes, Hassid determined that John's problem was a virus. Hassid explained to John that because his computer problem was virus related it was not covered under manufacturer warranty. From this point forward John would have to provide a credit card for billing for further support, which John assumed would be more script reading.

Unfortunately this type of problem and response is common in today's computer service world. Most computer problems are not covered under manufacturer or extended warranties and are the responsibility of the owner to get repaired.

If John cannot fix the problem he will either need to get help elsewhere or take the computer to a repair shop. John can expect to pay at least $100 for the repair and be without the computer for a few days.

Computer Repair Smartiepants was written for all the people tired of getting computer problems as described. Follow the instructions in this book and expect to stop paying computer shops for computer repairs. *Computer Repair Smartiepants* was written understanding that a non-technical frustrated computer user has four main concerns when they take their computer to a computer repair store for computer service:

- How much will the repair cost?
- How long will the repair take?
- Will data be lost?
- What can be done to prevent this from happening again?

A frustrated computer user doesn't understand or care that a computer technician had to edit the system registry, reset the web browser settings to correct an Internet problem or that hard drive permissions had to be removed to save important documents and files. The customer just wants the computer back working ASAP along with their important data saved.

Computer Repair Smartiepants is presented in easy to understand, non-technical terms. Most computer problems can be repaired without reading a manual or learning computer terminology. No need to learn boring computer techniques like how to edit a Windows registry or memorizing error messages and their meanings.

Computer Repair Smartiepants will give the reader a complete understanding of the computer troubleshooting process. The research techniques shown will allow troubleshooting virtually any type of problem - computers, home repairs, automotive and much more.

Topics covered include how diagnose and repair problems, how to prevent problems and how to get quality free help when encountering a problem that's too difficult. Never purchase another Dummies or computer help book again.

This book wasn't written to be a reference manual. Some important points and techniques are covered to help the reader retain and learn to use important methods when troubleshooting and repairing computers. This book will teach where and how to get help with problems too hard to solve on your own.

Computer Repair Smartiepants covers how to repair tablets, smart phones, printers, televisions and other electronic devices. We discuss the best free programs and websites and provide other useful computer tech tips.

Computer Repair Smartiepants is written in HYHY format. HYHY stands for **H**elp **Y**ou **H**elp **Y**ourself. Read this book carefully and apply the troubleshooting techniques and principles provided. Follow the principles in this book to repair over 85% of all computer problems without any help.

DISCLAIMERS

1. One week in the computer industry is like a year in other industries. Some material may become dated. On the positive side, most of the troubleshooting techniques presented in this book are still being used because they are still effective.

2. We primarily focused on troubleshooting techniques on computers using Windows. We do also cover problems with Apple and Android based equipment. The troubleshooting techniques discussed can be applied across all operating system platforms.

3. This book was written for seniors and basic computer novices or seniors that can follow basic instructions to fix their computers. This book was not written for computer techs searching for additional troubleshooting methods.

4. Some topics are covered more than one time. The reader should assume these points are very important.

Now let's get started.

1. WHY COMPUTER SUPPORT STINKS

The following true stories illustrate why computer users get frustrated with that dreaded yet indispensable electronic device we call a computer and the computer service industry.

Customer 1

A lady checks in her computer to my service department to replace a defective hard drive still under manufacturer warranty. I explained to her that our company was not authorized by the computer manufacturer to perform their warranty service. The manufacturer should provide her with a replacement part; however, she will have to pay my labor cost to install the drive and Windows. She told me that she would pay for the part and labor and to get started.

I asked her why she's coming to me instead of an authorized manufacturer service center. The computer manufacturer should repair her computer free of charge.

She replied that she was so frustrated dealing with the manufacturer that she would rather just take her computer to a computer repair shop and pay to get it repaired. She was on the phone with the manufacturer for hours diagnosing the problem.

The support rep was pleasant but spoke with a foreign accent so she had trouble understanding him. He had her run diagnostic tests. She had to wait on the phone for 30 minutes while the tests ran. He finally concluded that the hard drive was failing and needed to be replaced.

The support person wanted to ship her replacement hard drive and have her call back when the drive was received. A technician would then instruct her over the phone how to install the drive and re-install Windows. The process would take two to four hours. Before she could complain she was disconnected.

When she called back, she was told that she would have to re-start the entire troubleshooting process again from the beginning. At this point she just wanted to take the computer somewhere and pay someone to fix it.

Customer 2

A man checks in his notebook for a diagnostic. He just paid $90 for a diagnostic at a big box store. He was told that his notebook had a bad motherboard and the cost of the repair would be over $400. The manufacturer warranty expired two weeks prior to the problem and he wanted a second option.

I placed his notebook on the counter and tried to turn it on using his notebook AC charger and just using the battery. The notebook did not power up. I removed the battery from the notebook and attempted to turn on the notebook using the AC charger only. The notebook powered up with the battery removed from the notebook.

The problem was a defective battery causing the notebook not to turn on. His repair cost was $50 for a replacement battery instead of $400 for replacing a defective motherboard, which would not have corrected the problem anyway.

The customer was happy that we diagnosed a less expensive problem than he originally thought but upset that he paid $90 for a mis-diagnosed problem.

Customer 3

A senior calls to request an on-site service call. She recently had an onsite call from a competitor. The on-site technician found and removed viruses from her computer. After he finished, the computer still wasn't working properly. He then determined that Windows had to be re-installed.

She ended up paying $450 for the repair. The onsite technician charged her $200 for the onsite virus and spyware removal that didn't correct the problem. He charged her another $200 for a Windows operating system re-installation that did correct the problem. The service call was an additional $50.

Two weeks later her computer again had problems. The on-site company that performed the earlier work told her that if they came out again that the call and repair would be chargeable.

We picked up the computer at her home and took it back to our shop. We re-installed and updated Windows optimized the computer and installed free anti-virus and spyware removal programs and setup a backup so she could reset Windows herself guided by our instructions file if it became necessary.

We then returned the computer to her home and setup her system with her printer and Internet service. The repair was $150 for the service and an additional $69.99 for the pickup – drop-off service. This time she paid about ½ the price charged by an on-site company for a better job.

Customer 4

A lady checks in her desktop computer that has popups and won't access the Internet. It turns out that Windows was corrupted due to viruses. The virus removal and Windows repair attempts did not work, so her computer required a complete Windows re-installation.

She had photos on her hard drive that weren't backed up and very important to her. To save her photos we had to remove the drive from her computer and connect it to a different computer for a data transfer.

To complicate matters, her Windows user account was pass-word protected. Her data was "Permissioned" which meant that we had to remove password protection from her photos so they could be accessed. She ended up spending over $200 for the repair. Half the cost was for saving the photos that would not have been necessary if she had taken thirty seconds to copy the photos to an external USB flash drive.

Customer 5

A senior enters carrying a clipboard. His computer won't get on the Internet and he wanted to ask questions about how to repair the system. He purchased his computer elsewhere and apparently could not get his problem resolved through the other store or his Internet Service Provider support services.

I gave him advice on a couple of repair fixes to attempt and went back to work. He then approached another store employee and again begins to start a conversation.

I intervene and politely explain to the gentleman that since he didn't purchase a computer or receive service from us and we were not his Internet provider that he had the following options: he could bring his computer to the store and we could quickly test to see if his computer could get on the Internet with our Internet free of charge or we could dispatch a technician for on-site assistance.

The on-site call would be chargeable. When I suggested that he may want to either contact his Internet provider or where he purchased the computer to get further help, he cursed and left.

People have used Second Source Computers for 30 years to repair their computers. Usually we are used as a last resort and only after they've exhausted every other alternative. They know once they enter my store that unless they are under our maintenance contract or a senior, they will pay $59 for a diagnostic that goes towards the completed repair, data save or computer replacement if the computer is worth fixing.

My computer stores has diagnosed and repaired over 50,000 computers and electronic devices since 1988. We've worked on many computers over the years.

This is one of many local awards we've won. Every year we usually get voted first place for having the best Computer Service. We have won these awards because we provide superior computer service.

THE BAD NEWS

- Computer support and service is usually rated "poor" by surveyed customers.
- A growing number of computer problems are NOT covered under warranty.
- The average cost of a computer repair averages $150.
- In some cases, it can take weeks to get a computer repaired.

Back in the late 80's when 286 computers were selling for $2,000 with profit margins at 50%, computer companies and resellers would spend hours on the phone supporting customers.

Today with profit margins ranging between $25-50 on a new computer purchase, customers that require help with their computer usually end up calling the computer manufacturer directly, unless they purchased some type of support plan or extended warranty from the retail store.

Most computer customer service is outsourced outside the United States. The support people can be hard to understand. Once a customer finally gets to speak with a human, the first phone contact will be with a Level One Representative. A level one support technician usually isn't very knowledgeable.

A Level One support person usually reads from a script for every problem. If the problem is difficult, the customer may have to endure a gauntlet of two or three support people and hours on hold before reaching someone that can actually help with the problem. Or worse yet, a customer can be on the phone for hours and get disconnected or not get the problem resolved.

Onsite service is worse. People may pay up to triple the price for an on-site service call and the job will not be performed as well. A virus removal or Windows re-installation done properly can take an entire day to complete.

Ask an on-site computer company what they charge for a complete Windows re-installation. A complete Windows installation should be downloading and installing all Windows and device driver updates, followed by a system optimization. Include installation of anti-virus, spyware removal, word-processing and setup of their printer and then finish with a complete system image. Their price most likely will be higher than originally quoted.

Big box stores have in-store computer repair service centers. In some cases, these service departments accept a customer's money for diagnostic they know that they cannot repair in store.

Their primary mission is to advise the customer to replace instead of repairing the broken system. It's easier to push a new system out the door than to fix a broken one.

Computers are unlike any other type of electronic device. In most cases an LCD TV, DVD, phone, gaming devices, and other electronic items either work or they don't. If they stop working, it's usually because of a hardware problem and either the item is under warranty or it isn't.

If a computer isn't working, the odds are almost 85% that the problem is software or user caused and will not be repaired under warranty. So, there are two choices – get someone to fix the problem or fix the problem yourself.

The problem is that today with almost 85% of the problems being software related, replacing a computer doesn't necessarily mean that the same type of software problem won't reoccur on the replacement system.

Computer Repair Smartiepants will give all necessary information to diagnose and repair most computers. The question is how much effort the reader wants to learn computer troubleshooting and take matters into your own hands.

The successful technicians in this business aren't necessarily the most technical or the smartest. The best technicians know where to research the problem to find the solution. If nothing else, anyone that follows these troubleshooting techniques will be able to repair computers without help.

Follow the troubleshooting principles in this book and stop paying for computer service.

2. ALWAYS ASSUME THIS

Take this to the bank. You can take every precautionary step possible; however, at some point your computer will crash. You can live a good life; say your prayers every day, follow every golden rule and it all doesn't matter. Someday, sometime, somewhere your computer is going to crash. Perhaps a power surge caused the problem. Maybe clicking on a link caused the problem. Perhaps Windows just decided today was the day for the computer to crash. Whatever the cause, the computer isn't working properly. Understand it's not IF your system will crash, **but WHEN**. The key is to be prepared for the when.

Assume that your computer will crash. Get prepared for that day NOW, not when it happens.

3. THE THREE GOLDEN RULES

Computer repair centers exist for the same reason car service centers exist - people pay to have their computers repaired because either:

- They can't do it themselves.
- Their time or getting the computer repaired quickly is worth the cost.

Computer repair shops still exist because they repair non-warranted computer problems. Most non-warranty problems are caused by software. Software is a collection of computer programs and related data that provide the instructions for telling a computer what to do and how to do it.

Most manufacturer warranties exclude software problems. Viruses, spyware, corrupt Windows, many Windows blue screen errors, web-browser and popups are all examples of software problems. Software problems account for over 85% of all computer problems.

DISPOSABLE SOCIETY

We live in a disposable society. We consume, use and dispose of our electronic items. It's much easier to dispose of our problematic electronic items and purchase replacements.

Most computers today have about ½ the life that they had 10 years ago. The obsolesce is based on two factors: the ability of the market to deliver electronic items at a lower price and the software operating system upgrades that consistently require more powerful computers. People with computer problems are conscious that computers are less inexpensive when deciding whether to get a computer repaired.

Most computers can be repaired by anyone that follows the following rules:

THREE GOLDEN RULES

85% of all computer problems can be repaired if the following steps are taken:

1. *Learn how to re-install Windows (or other operating system).*
2. *Backup important files to a cloud location or external storage device separate from the computer.*
3. *Use only freeware or legally purchased software.*

WHY FOLLOW THESE RULES?

Follow these three rules for preventing and repairing any software problem, which account for 85% of all computer problems. Virus, spy ware or malware problem? Can't get on the Internet? Blue screens? Corrupt Windows? Re-install Windows, replace your programs and data and move on.

If 85% of computer problems are software caused and re-installingWindows corrects most of these problems, doesn't it make sense to at least attempt a re-installation prior to taking the computer to service?

Many people will bring their computers in for service because they do not know how to re-install Windows or do not have a backup of their data. Why people bring their computers to a service center in the first place:

REASONS FOR NOT FOLLOWING THE GOLDEN RULES

1. LACK OF KNOWLEDGE

Many computers only require a single or couple of keystrokes to install Windows. Windows provides an option to restore Windows and save the user files on the system.

Anyone that wants to be free from paying for computer service should learn how to re-install Windows on their Windows-based systems. This advice holds true even if using a Google Chrome book or Mac. Figure out how to re-install the operating system.

2. MISSING THE NECESSARY RECOVERY MEDIA

Most new computers do not include recovery media. Many systems require a specific keystroke on startup to begin a Windows recovery process. New systems should allow the user to make a complete image backup or make a bootable backup media device for Windows re-installation.

3. DATA LOSS

People are afraid that if Windows is re-installed the programs and important data will be lost. Learn to back-up important files and data from the computer, this reason should not be an issue.

4. PROGRAM LOSS

Everyone has a friend, relative or co-worker that has installed programs on a computer that weren't legally purchased. Get in the habit of using only legally purchased software or freeware programs that are easily downloadable.

The single most stolen program illegally installed onto a user's computer is Microsoft Office. There are freeware office suites that can provide the Office functionality, but if Microsoft Office is necessary then purchase it.

Most people just require Microsoft Word. Word can be purchased separately for under $100. Academic institutions and non-profit organizations typically receive discounts from Microsoft.

5. RE-INSTALLING WINDOWS IS TOO MUCH WORK

A Windows re-installation takes time because all Windows updates have to be retrieved online and that can take hours to days. The process to begin an initial re-installation may only be a couple of minutes once learned.

Acquiring and completing all Windows updates is another matter. The initial re-installation process many only take 1-2 hours, but updates can take a day or two to complete. It is strongly advised to get all Windows updates for security reasons.

Consider the alternative. Our techs sometimes spend a day removing viruses, spyware and malware and after all that work determine that Windows needs to be re-installed anyway.

Factor in the time to disconnect the computer, take it down the steps to the car, check it into service and have to pick it back up. Remember the service will cost money and there will be down time without the computer.

Learn to install your computer operating system, keep important files backed up and have legal access to your programs and there isn't a computer problem that you cannot recover from.

Following the Three Golden Rules, will enable a recovery from most computer problems.

4. HARDWARE OR SOFTWARE?

Who cares if the problem is hardware or software? The computer's not working and it needs to get repaired.

The cause of the problem can make a big difference and here's why. <u>If the problem is hardware and the computer is under manufacturer warranty the problem should be repaired without any cost to the owner.</u> How much hassle and how quickly it gets repaired may be an issue, but it should not cost any money.

If the computer is not under warranty correcting the problem is on the user whether the problem is hardware or software. Software problems aren't covered by anyone and <u>don't expect any software repair to be free, even if the computer is under warranty.</u>

If the problem is software related the problem can be solved by re-installing Windows and it will not cost anything if done by the user.

HARDWARE BIOS SYSTEM TEST

Most computer manufacturers have system tests located in the SYSTEM SETUP OR BIOS to test for problems with the computer hardware. To access these testing programs, get into the BIOS or SYSTEM on startup. The Bios programs are prior to loading Windows. To access the System Bios, press the F2, F1 or DELETE key on startup.

If unsure whether the problem is hardware or software related, attempt a Windows re-installation. If a Windows re-installation corrects the problem, the problem was a software problem. If not, the problem most likely is hardware-related.

Hardware problems are usually noisy or video related.

If a computer is beeping or noisy, the problem is probably hardware related. Beeps, knocks, whirls, any type of new noise that wasn't there earlier is a probable indication that the problem is hardware, not software.

IT'S PROBABLY A HARDWARE PROBLEM

1. No power to the computer or monitor.
2. Computer makes unusual noises when turned on or running.
3. The computer is burning or smoking.
4. The computer or monitor power light is on, but no video.
5. The computer beeps but does not turn on.
6. The computer makes a clacking sound (bad hard drive).
7. Error messages indicating a hardware problem for example "Data error reading drive C" "hard drive imminent failure" or "Memory problem".

SYMPTOMS OF HARWARE PROBLEM

The following system problems would indicate a problem with the following hardware:

1. ENTIRE SYSTEM SLOW
   The entire system is slow from starting up, loading Windows and both on and off the Internet; the hard drive may be failing.

2. SYSTEM RECYCLES
   The computer recycles or the system has "weird" problems that are hard to trace look at the hard drive or memory.

3. VIDEO FLASHING or DISCOLORED SCREEN
   The problem still persists after changing video settings and swapping monitors doesn't work look at video card or onboard video.

4. WINDOWS DOESN'T RECOGNIZE A DEVICE – CD ROM, NETWORK CARD, or MODEM
   The problem may be with that particular part.

IT'S PROBABLY A SOFTWARE PROBLEM

1. Computer intermittently "BLUE SCREENS".
2. Computer runs Windows in SAFE MODE only.
3. DLL error messages on startup.
4. Popups appear when on Internet.
5. Computer begins to run slower, but no hard drive errors.
6. A Windows error message that doesn't refer to hardware.
7. Anything else.

Where ever possible, attempt a full Windows or other operating system re-installation. Most likely the re-installation will correct the problem and since the data is backed up, all is well.

Hardware problems are usually more noisy and power or video related. Software problems are usually everything else.

5. SOFTWARE PROBLEMS

We introduced the concept of computer problems falling into a classification of either hardware or software. This chapter will discuss the differences in more detail.

BUG or GLITCH

A bug or glitch is used to describe an error or mistake in a computer program or system that produces an incorrect result or problem with a computer program. Most software bugs arise from mistakes and errors made by the programmers that wrote the program.

A software problem can exist with Windows or an application program isn't working. Bugs are responsible for software problems.

TYPES OF SOFTWARE PROBLEMS

1. WINDOWS ISSUES

There is no such as the bug free operating system – it doesn't exist. Operating system errors can include dll files missing, cab files being overwritten, the "Blue Screen of death" or Windows just not starting or closing properly.

2. WINDOWS CORRUPTION DUE TO HARDWARE PROBLEM

Windows can get corrupted because of a hardware problem. The defective part can be replaced and Windows still won't work properly. Why?

This may help explain Windows corruption. Assume you sprained an ankle and for the next couple of weeks had to use a cane to aid in walking. After a couple of weeks of cane use, the lower back opposite your bad ankle begins to hurt.

The new pain is a result of over compensating the rest of your body to avoid placing too much pressure on the problem ankle. A secondary problem has now developed as compensation directly related to the primary problem.

Windows had to overcompensate for whatever hardware problem the system experienced. Improper shutdowns, fluctuations in power, overheating, and all these issues can corrupt Windows. It's best to re-install Windows with a full hard drive format when Windows corruption takes place.

Windows can cause problems with its own updates. Sad but true. Microsoft usually will setup a backup on the computer receiving updates in case there is a problem.

3. APPLICATION PROGRAM PROBLEMS

Windows may be working. The problem could be with an application program. An application program is any non-Windows operating system program. It could be a word-processing program, accounting, video editing or any non-Windows program.

Microsoft Office is an application program, which is separate from the Windows operating system. Adobe Photoshop, Quicken, QuickBooks, Turbo Tax, and computer games are examples of application programs.

Application programs like any software can have bugs. Application programs may not work for the same reasons that Windows may not work – a program or Windows update or a conflict with another application running on the computer, incompatible software versions are reasons an application may not work.

Read a software license agreement. Legally, the software company isn't liable for anything. Use software at your own risk. If the company that developed the product won't assume responsibility, why should any computer store repair a software problem without charging?

Hardware manufacturers warrant their products for a period of time. If the system fails under warranty the manufacturer will either repair the problem or replace the system. If a bug in the software causes a problem with the computer, "Oh, well sorry", "We can fix it but it will be chargeable" or repair it yourself.

USER-CAUSED PROBLEM

A user-caused problem is with the user operation of the equipment and not the equipment itself. A user-caused problem is when the user did not properly use the equipment or program. A user problem usually means that the user may require computer training.

Examples of user-caused problems:

- A virus or other destructive program was placed onto the computer.
- Water was spilled onto the keyboard.
- Someone tripped over the power cord and damaged the unit.
- A flash drive is connected to a USB computer port causing the computer to not turn on.
- A notebook was dropped and the screen cracked.
- A downloaded program also caused other destructive programs to download and negatively impact the computer.

85% of all computer problems are software or user caused.

The number is probably higher. People don't want to spend money to get their computer cleaned of viruses, spy ware and junk files and would rather run their computer at less than full capacity then to shell out money and be without their computer for a while.

SOFTWARE PROBLEM CAUSES

The main reasons for software problems are:

1. Viruses, spy ware, and malware.
2. Conflict between programs or hardware and software.
3. Windows corruption.
4. Bad programming.

VIRUSES AND SPYWARE

I get asked by people what they can do to avoid getting viruses and spy ware. They hate my answer; however, I stand by it. I tell them the only sure way to avoid viruses, spyware and malware is to not use the Internet. Over 20,000 new viruses, spyware and malware files are released weekly and it takes weeks to months for removal tools to get developed for release.

It's impossible to run any anti-virus program that protects against every virus, spyware and malware file released on the Internet. The anti-virus companies develop removal tools and browser patch security holes as quickly as they can; however, there will always be lag time between when the new destructive files hit the Internet and when the security updates and removal tools are released for online downloading.

PROGRAM CONFLICTS

Sometimes different programs don't get along. A program conflict occurs when two programs cannot co-exist or run on the same computer. It is due to a programming bug and usually occurs when the two programs fight for the same computer resource such as a memory location. Sometimes a hardware device driver software update or program update can cause Windows not to work correctly.

WINDOWS UPDATES

Windows updates can be a source of a system crash; especially when Windows attempts to update hardware device drivers. Windows usually will setup a restore point prior to updating. The restore point can be used to recover in case of an update problem.

WINDOWS CORRUPTION

Sometimes Windows just gets corrupted. Windows corruption means that Windows doesn't work properly. Windows corruption can be caused by anything from a failing hard drive to any reason listed above. Corrupted Windows usually requires a re-installation of Windows.

BAD PROGRAMMING

There's very little a consumer can do about poor programming. Limit exposure by not being the first person to purchase a new program or download. Wait to purchase and use new software or download a major service pack upgrade. Follow this advice for other electronic devices such as smart phones or tablets. Wait on downloading and installing that software update.

WARRANTY

Software issues are not covered under manufacturer warranty. Would you take your brand new car back to the car manufacturer for free work if you got into an accident? Learn how to repair computer software problems or you will be paying someone to handle the problem for you.

Most problems are software or user caused and not covered under manufacturer warranty.

6. BASIC HARDWARE REPAIR

When we refer to basic hardware repair, our discussion will center on computer desktops and some notebook repairs.

INSIDE A COMPUTER

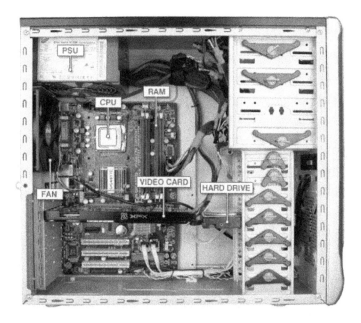

This is the inside of a desktop computer system. Computers don't have many parts. Most computer hardware problems are corrected by replacing one of five components:

1. Power supply
2. Hard Drive
3. Memory
4. Video Card
5. Motherboard

Notice that we used the word "replace", not "repair". It's less expensive to replace rather than repair most computer hardware.

Some parts are easier to replace than others; replacing a power supply, memory or video card is much easier than replacing a motherboard. Replacing a motherboard is one job to either avoid or delegate because it can be time consuming.

Replacing a hard drive can be time consuming because Windows will have to be re-installed on the replacement drive. When a new or used hard drive is purchased, it should be a clean drive, meaning all data including any prior operating system should be wiped off the drive entirely.

SWAP PARTS TO TEST

Most hardware problems are diagnosed by swapping a suspect part with a working part to check a problem. Follow these steps to swap out parts to test a hardware problem:

1. Disconnect all cables and connections connected to the computer.
2. Move the computer to an appropriate workplace with proper lighting, space and power.
3. Have a Phillips head or flat head screwdriver.
4. Touch metal to ground yourself prior to opening the computer case.
5. Open the case.
6. Review all connections.
7. Remove the part and install the replacement.
8. If possible, attempt to test the computer prior to replacing the computer cover.
9. If the part works, reassemble the computer and load the software driver for the new replacement part.

The question then becomes how much time to spend taking a computer apart, swapping parts until diagnosing the problem part, re-installing a working part, updating drivers and possibly re-installing Windows? Is your time worth the effort?

TYPES OF HARDWARE PROBLEMS

1. System overheating.
2. Power supply
3. Hard drive
4. Motherboard
5. Memory
6. Video card
7. CPU
8. Mouse
9. Keyboard
10. External Devices

SYSTEM OVERHEATING

The most common hardware problem is a system overheating. Overheating can be caused by a part failing; however, dust build-up inside the system and blocked air vents are the usual primary culprit. Heat problems will be discussed in more detail later.

POWER SUPPLY

Our local power company keeps us in business. We usually get half dozen systems with blown power supplies after a storm. We stock different types of power supplies because power problems are frequent. Power supplies can be blown because the user doesn't have a good surge protector attached to the system.

HARD DRIVE

Older SATA hard drives have moving parts. Any item with moving parts will eventually break. A hard drive isn't difficult to replace; however, Windows will need to be re-installed on the replacement hard drive. Re-installation shouldn't be too difficult with system recovery media. Without system recovery media, a replacement set or recovery DVDs or flash drive may have to be purchased online.

MOTHERBOARD

Motherboards are the lifeblood of any computer and can be affected by a power surge. Only the really technically oriented should attempt a motherboard repair or replacement. Anyone considering this repair should first research online for information. The manufacturer website and YouTube are good places to start.

MEMORY

Failing memory or memory not properly seated is a common hardware problem. A memory problem is frequently indicated in a startup error message. Attempt to reseat the memory prior to replacing it. Sometimes reseating memory will correct the problem. Adding or upgrading memory is a fairly easy job and shouldn't take much time.

VIDEO CARD

Video cards are one computer part that higher end users and gamers upgrade for better performance. Video cards and on-board video can fail. If an on-motherboard video card fails, a separate video card can be inserted into an open motherboard slot. Installing a separate video card isn't a very time consuming process.

CPU

It's very rare that the CPU fails. Chips can run hot if they are over processing for greater speed performance (overclocked), the chip cooling fan stops working or the thermal paste wears out which helps keep the CPU cool.

MOUSE & KEYBOARD

A flakey mouse or keyboard can cause a computer not to work properly. Keyboards and mice are inexpensive. Keep a backup of each for testing. With a wireless mouse or keyboard, try replacing the batteries first.

EXTERNAL DEVICES

Peripheral devices connected to a computer may cause a computer not to work. A defective printer, multipass unit, external router / modem, card reader, or other device can cause the computer to not work properly. Disconnect all external devices from the computer and test the device on a different system to isolate the problem.

RE-INSTALL WINDOWS BEFORE SWAPPING HARDWARE

I once had a tech that worked for me whose answer to every problem was to re-install Windows. Blue screen? Re-install Windows. Pop-ups? Re-install Windows. Error reading hard drive? Re-install Windows. Device driver problem? Re-install Windows.

This tech would re-install Windows to repair a car if possible. He couldn't repair any complicated software problem; however, his bench was always cleared and his customers didn't complain. They were happy to get their computers back and working properly in a timely manner.

Obviously re-installing Windows doesn't correct every problem and there can be draw backs re-installing Windows for certain problems. Re-installing Windows should correct most software problems and if the problem isn't corrected, at least you now know that the problem is hardware related.

OPEN AND LOOK FIRST

Study the repair to attempt. Make notes on how things are connected and what slots cards in located, and what screws go where. Make sure to take notes on the disassembly so the computer can be put back together again.

BASIC HARDWARE REPAIR CHECKLIST

1. Ground yourself prior to working on the computer by touching metal.
2. Disconnect all cables from the computer.
3. Move the computer to an appropriate work area for opening.
4. Open the case.
5. If the computer has a dust buildup, take outside and compress air clean it.
6. Check for loose cables.
7. Push firmly on all cables, cards and memory to check that all are seated properly.
8. Reconnect the computer and restart the computer.

1. WORKSPACE

Make sure the workspace is appropriate for taking apart a computer. The table should be large enough to place an open computer, monitor and loose parts. Check that there is ample lighting to find screws when they drop on the ground. Check that the work area is clear. The table should be clear except for the replacement parts to install. If possible, work in a non-rug covered environment. Walking on a rug builds up static electricity within your body that can damage a computer.

2. TOOLS

Have a good Phillips head screwdriver. If working with Mac equipment a special set of star tipped screwdrivers will be required. A notebook requires a set of smaller screwdrivers. Have either a can of compressed air or a vacuum cleaner to clean up dust. Certain manufacturers use a proprietary star-shaped bit that requires a different type screwdriver.

3. TOUCH METAL

Touch metal prior to opening a desktop. Touching metal will dissipate any stored static electricity within your body. Static electricity does not mix with computer parts.

4. POWER

Check that the unit isn't powered on or connected to a power outlet.

ONCE THE CASE IS OPEN

1. AIR COMPRESS CLEAN

First blow forced air to compress clean the computer from dust buildup. Heat issues from dust buildup can cause hardware problems. Eliminate that possibility as a potential problem right off the bat. Shoot compressed air through each opening in the power supply and focus on the CPU, the CPU fan and memory.

2. PRESS ON ALL CARDS AND CONNECTIONS

While grounded, press on each card and cable connections. Press on the memory and hard drive cable connections. SATA drive cables get loose easier than the older IDE ribbon type cables. Press on the CPU and CPU fan to check that the fan is properly attached to the CPU chip.

REPLACING PC PARTS

Parts are either replaced because the old part failed or replaced because the part is being upgraded. Follow these steps for either reason:

1. DEVICE MANAGER

First disable or uninstall the part being replaced in DEVICE MANAGER in Windows. By disabling the old device prior to installing the new device, the potential for device conflicts is lessened.

2. FOLLOW THE RULES

Follow the prior instructions about the work area; ground yourself and remove the cover.

3. REMOVE AND REPLACE

When replacing a card and the replacement card uses the same card slot, insert the replacement card in the slot. Replace the screw holding the card in place.

4. INSTALL THE NEW HARDWARE DRIVER AND TEST

Restart the computer. If possible restart the computer without replacing the side panel because if the repair didn't work, the side cover will have to be removed again. If the computer turns on, Windows will find the new hardware. Next install the manufacturer-provided driver. If everything works, shut the computer off and replace the computer side panel.

SHUT DOWN FIXES

Above is a shot of the famous "Blue Screen of Death" when Windows goes bonkers. The screen will say something like "Windows has shut down to prevent further damage to the computer" and list all kinds of line and code information.

WHAT CAUSES SHUTDOWN PROBLEMS?

Heat is the major cause of any computer shutdown. Usually a shutdown issue is caused when a component in the computer is overheating. The computer either shuts itself off automatically to prevent damage or Windows blue screens.

The computer can shut itself completely off without notice. These are variations of what we call a Windows Shut down Problem. If a computer powers down after running for 10 minutes or longer, the computer may have an overheating problem.

When the CPU is getting too hot and the SYSTEM sensors react to the overheating by shutting down the computer to protect the computer from heat damage. A computer or Windows shut down problem is a very common hardware problem.

CPU HEAT PROBLEMS

The most common type of shutdown problem is with the CPU. Check the following:

1. **CHECK THE HEAT SINK**

   Remove the CPU heat sink from the CPU. The heat sink is the coolant device on top of the CPU. BE CAREFUL when working with the CPU. Watch a YouTube video online to see how to properly remove a heat sink.

2. **CLEAN THE CPU**

   First check that the CPU is clean. Wipe off any old paste and crud. Clean the CPU thoroughly with a dry cloth.

3. **APPLY THERMAL PASTE**

   See if there's any thermal paste between the CPU and heat sink or fan. The thermal paste helps keep the CPU cool by dissipating heat from the CPU and to the heat sink. Purchase thermal paste and apply on the CPU. Apply liberally and reseat the CPU.

OTHER SHUT DOWN POSSIBILITIES

Other causes for a shutdown problem:

1. **FLAKEY POWER SUPPLY**

   A failing power supply can cause a computer to shut down. Connect a test replacement power supply and test.

2. **BAD MEMORY OR BAD MEMORY SLOT**

   If a memory slot is bad and there is an open slot, switch the memory to the free slot. If the shut downs still continue, try replacement memory.

3. RESET BIOS DEFAULTS

Perhaps the sensor settings are not setup properly and resetting the system settings may correct that particular problem. Get into the System Setup and LOAD SYSTEM DEFAULTS. That will reset the system settings back to factory default.

4. POWER / ENVIRONMENTAL

Perhaps the electrical socket has too much draw. Move the computer to a different room or connect the computer to a UPS. A UPS provides uninterrupted and more level power flow to a device in case the power cuts out.

MOTHERBOARD REPLACEMENT

A motherboard replacement is the ultimate of all hardware repairs. It's the PC techs equivalent of a car mechanic building a Formula One racecar. A tech that can successfully replace a motherboard can pretty much repair any computer hardware problem.

Weigh the benefits and drawbacks of performing a motherboard replacement before tackling it. Most manufacturer desktop and notebook computers will require that particular manufacturer make and model replacement part and the part may be expensive relative to replacing the system. The part may cost up to 50% of the replacement cost of a new computer.

Assuming the cost is not an objection. Assume at least a half of a day's work. So many things can go wrong. The board wasn't seated properly. The board is shorting out the system. The CPU chip wasn't properly replaced. Even if the repair works, there's still more to do.

The repair can be completed and then later discover that Windows won't activate. Windows may see the system to be activated as a different computer with the same Windows license. Even replacing an exact motherboard can be seen as a change to the Microsoft activation servers. Microsoft will have to be contacted to explain the problem and request a phone activation of the system.

We rarely perform motherboard replacements today because the cost to replace a motherboard parts plus the time it takes is too close to the cost of replacing the system with a new computer.

SEARCH ONLINE FOR A VIDEO PRIOR TO STARTING ANY ADVANCED COMPUTER SYSTEM REPAIR.

First check YouTube. For example, to replace a notebook screen, enter the make and model of the notebook followed by "notebook screen replacement" and see what "How to Videos" is available.

Get creative and enter a more specific search using the notebook make and model number followed by the part to replace such as "keyboard replacement", "screen replacement" or another specific repair. Any sharp repair person will get background information on the type of repair they're going to attempt, prior to attacking it.

NOTEBOOK REPAIRS

A good notebook technician is organized and has patience. Impatient people should not attempt to disassemble a notebook because the odds are that it won't get back together properly.

NOTEBOOK MEMORY

Replacing or upgrading notebook memory isn't difficult if the notebook memory slot is on the bottom of the unit. Some newer models require the entire notebook to be taken apart, which is very stupid design work. Assuming the memory slot is on the bottom and easily accessible:

1. Make sure there is no power to the unit and remove the battery.
2. Touch metal to dissipate any static charge from your body.
3. Turn the notebook upside down and look for a compartment that is labeled "MEM" or "Memory" or a symbol that represents memory.
4. Use a small Phillips head screwdriver to open the cover.
5. Be careful if removing old memory. The memory brackets need to be moved to release the memory for removal. Don't break the slot connectors holding the memory in place or the slot won't be usable.
6. Snap in the replacement memory and turn on the notebook. If the memory is correct, the notebook will acknowledge the change in memory size on startup. If the memory isn't the right type, the notebook will beep and there probably won't be any video. Shut the notebook down and reseat the computer memory. Also try different memory in each slot in case there's a problem with a memory slot.

HARD DRIVE

A replacement hard drive first needs to be installed, then the operating system must be re-installed from scratch.

1. Make sure there is no power to the unit and remove the battery.
2. Touch metal to dissipate any static charge from your body.
3. Turn the notebook upside down and look for the location that houses the hard drive.
4. Remove the screws with a Philips head screwdriver and remove the hard drive.
5. If the unit has to be disassembled to install the hard drive, find a video on YouTube showing the repair process.
6. The hard drive will be enclosed in a caddie. Remove the caddie screws to release the hard drive.
7. The drive may have a special adapter connected. Remove the adapter.
8. Insert the replacement in the caddie and replace the screws. There is no reason to tighten the screws as tight as possible.
9. Re-insert the hard drive back into the notebook.
10. Start the system and begin a Windows re-installation.

LCD SCREEN

A notebook screen gets replaced because the screen failed or was damaged. Replacing a notebook screen in most cases isn't all that difficult. Make sure the screen is the only problem with the notebook prior to ordering a replacement screen.

First connect the notebook to an external monitor through the notebook HDMI or VGA port and check that the screen is the problem and the only problem. The same trauma that caused the screen to crack could have damaged the hard drive or other component. Reconsider a screen repair if the notebook has other issues besides a broken screen.

OBTAINING REPLACEMENT PARTS

Check Amazon or EBay first for replacement parts if nothing else to get an idea of pricing. My customers order their own notebook replacement screens online and bring the screen and notebook to me for the repair when the screen arrives. This process saves them money and if the wrong screen is shipped (it happens) they aren't angry at me.

Before purchasing review the seller warranty and return policy. Make sure that the part can be returned or exchanged if it's the incorrect part. Pay by PayPal or a credit card so there is recourse if there is a problem.

REMOVING A NOTEBOOK SCREEN

To remove and replace the notebook screen, the screen frame or bezel has to be taken apart. Different makes and models have their nuances, so look for a video showing how to remove the make and model notebook to work on. Check the manufacturer website for detailed specifications. Check YouTube for a video for additional technical support help.

Once the screws are removed and the frame removed, the next step is to disconnect the power and signal cable from the screen and remove the screen from the unit. Install the replacement screen and only replace a couple of screws to hold the screen in place. Turn the notebook back on to check the work. Always check the repair prior to replacing the screws.

NOTEBOOK AC JACK

A notebook jack gets damaged when someone trips over the power cord connected to the notebook. The trauma pulling or pushing on the jack separates the jack from the main board inside the notebook.

A jack repair is arguably the most difficult notebook repair. Many newer jacks are what are called "tethered", meaning that it connects by clipping a small cable to the motherboard, a much easier repair.

Older notebooks require a re-soldering of a jack. Soldering isn't required with newer notebooks using tethered jacks because a tethered jack just snaps into pin outs on the motherboard. Check the make and model of notebook online to determine the type of jack required.

The notebook must be disassembled to get to the motherboard; however, the motherboard doesn't necessarily have to be completely removed from the unit. There will be anywhere between 20-50 screws to remove to get to a notebook motherboard. Reseat the new jack, re-assemble the notebook and test.

Determine whether it's worth your time to get involved with hardware repairs.

7. THE BIGGEST ADVANTAGE COMPUTER STORES HAVE

"Diagnosing a computer hardware problem isn't rocket science. Just keep swapping parts until the computer works again."

Me – at least 1,000 times over 30 years

Most people probably believe the biggest advantage a computer store has is the knowledge and technical ability of the techs. People probably think that computer stores have all these super-duper techie programs that instantly diagnose and repair most computer problems. Guess again.

All the computer smarts in the world aren't much value without having MULTIPLE PARTS for testing purposes.

We stock multiple types of power supplies, video cards, memory, mice, keyboards, monitors, and other parts. You name it and we probably have it. Having replacement parts for testing is what separates a computer store from the home or small business user.

Hardware problems are usually caused by one of six parts: power supply, hard drive, memory, video card / monitor or motherboard.

THE ADVANTAGES OF HAVING MULTIPLE PARTS

Listed below are some common hardware problems that are easy to test with replacement parts.

MONITOR DOESN'T SHOW AN IMAGE

The problem could be with the LCD monitor or the video card within the computer. A technician can quickly isolate the problem by testing the computer with a different monitor. If a different monitor doesn't display an image, the problem is probably with the computer. Borrow a different monitor from another system in the house or see one can be borrowed from work or a neighbor for testing.

MOUSE OR KEYBOARD DOESN'T WORK

Is it a problem with the mouse or keyboard or the computer? First try the same mouse or keyboard in a different USB port. If that doesn't work, use a different mouse or keyboard. Having an extra mouse or keyboard for testing will help isolate the problem quickly.

NO POWER TO COMPUTER

First check the power to the outlet and the outlet itself. Assuming power supply is working, next step is to check the computer.

Remove the side cover of a desktop computer, disconnect the computer power supply and connect a test power supply to the motherboard. If the computer begins to start up, the power supply in the computer is probably blown and needs to be replaced. A power supply is a repair worth getting done assuming the power supply is the only problem.

If the computer doesn't turn on with a test power supply, the computer may have a motherboard problem or worse yet a blown power supply and motherboard. Any motherboard related problem probably is not worth the time or expense to repair.

NOTEBOOK / LAPTOP NOT POWERING UP

A universal AC charger with multiple tips is can be a convenient testing tool. If your notebook doesn't power up, remove the battery first and turn on without the battery. If nothing happens, power up the notebook using a different AC charger.

PARTS FOR TESTING

In addition to the parts listed above, these parts can help take PC troubleshooting to the next level.

POWER SUPPLY AND TESTER

A new power supply for testing purposes may cost $25. A power supply tester can give an indication of whether the power supply is good, but a power supply tester isn't 100% accurate. A power supply tester costs $10.

TEST CARDS

A test video card can be useful to test video problems. A system may have problems with an onboard video; however, a replacement video card may correct the problem. Check the available video slot in the desktop. Most slots on a motherboard should have a PCI-Express video slot. A test video card should cost: $10-15 used; $30-50 new.

DVD DRIVE

A test DVD drive should be kept to test optical drive problems and to install software if necessary. A SATA interface DVD-RW drive should cost: $10-15 used; $30-40 new.

HARD DRIVE

A test hard drive with a Windows operating system installed is a nice testing tool. If a computer isn't loading into Windows, disconnect the drive and connect the test drive. If the computer loads into Windows, the problem is with the drive or Windows operating system. A used hard drive for testing may cost $20 or more. Windows should be installed on the drive for testing purposes.

MEMORY

To operate a computer store to keep different types of memory in stock for testing purposes. Memory problems can be tested by reseating memory, testing memory sticks one by one in different memory slots.

BOOTABLE DEVICES

A boot device installs a program that makes a computer work. Devices that can start or boot a computer can be boot disks or boot drives which normally could be a hard drive, but also could be a USB flash drive, or DVD.

The bootable device has software that will allow the computer to start to that device. The software could have Windows or some form of testing software. A bootable flash drive or DVD is a necessity if Windows doesn't load from the hard drive. A tech can run diagnostic tests, check for viruses, recover data and even occasionally correct the problem using a program from the bootable media.

A repair disk is a bootable version of Windows or other operating system that installs from the boot device into the computer memory. A bootable device is needed when the computer hard drive will not load Windows properly on the computer's initial start-up.

CHKDSK REPAIR

CHKDSK is a command on computers running in Windows that displays the file system integrity status of hard drive and fix logical file system errors. A Chkdsk repair can fix many Windows problems and is a good program to run if Windows doesn't work properly. Boot up using either Active or Ultimate Boot Disk and run either a CHKDSK Repair or HARD DRIVE Repair program.

MASTER BOOT RECORD FIX

What is the MBR? MBR stands for Master Boot Record and it's the first sector on the hard drive tells the BIOS where to look for the operating system on the computer. If the MBR becomes damaged or corrupt, then the operating system will be unable to load. Common messages with this type of problem show error messages like:

- Error loading operating system
- Missing operating system
- Invalid partition table

Programs will fix master boot record problems such as Active Disk, Hirems, Ultimate Boot CD and others. If the system demonstrates this type of problem, consider a full Windows re-installation rather than attempting to repair this type of problem with a repair. Running a check disk repair program will not hurt the computer.

USB BOOTABLE OPERATING SYSTEM

Keep a copy of your computer's operating system on either a USB or DVD (assuming the computer has a DVD drive). Make sure the USB or DVD is bootable, which means allowing the computer to start from either the DVD or USB device.

Computer stores have multiple parts for testing. Consider keeping extra parts around for testing purposes.

8. HOW TO TROUBLESHOOT ANY PROBLEM

The answer to every question on any topic is available? Everyone has instant access to the most powerful research tool and extensive library in the world. This tip places the reader on equal footing with the most experienced computer tech in the world when it comes to solving a hard computer problem.

Use THE INTERNET to Google (or other search engine) to troubleshoot <u>any</u> problem.

how to disable	
how to disable uac	544,000 results
how to disable firewall	567,000 results
how to disable mcafee	656,000 results
how to disable avg	1,280,000 results
how to disable system restore	590,000 results
how to disable autorun	304,000 results
how to disable norton	1,190,000 results
how to disable windows defender	539,000 results
how to disable selinux	76,500 results
how to disable cookies	1,250,000 results
	close

GOOGLE THE PROBLEM

All that's necessary to diagnose any computer problem is a computer and the Internet to access the most comprehensive library ever created.

Error code X8YBC? Registry error at line 113? Program shutdown at line 13332? What's that mean? Perform an Internet search to find the answer to any computer problem. We call this method of searching **Googling the problem**.

Google is the most used Internet search engine. A browser search engine is similar to using a library card index. Googling the problem means using Google (or different search engine) to research a problem on the Internet.

TO GOOGLE A PROBLEM:

1. Get on the Internet.
2. Log on to Google.
3. Enter a brief description of the type of problem and press the ENTER key.

USING GOOGLE TO RESEARCH PROBLEMS

1. ERROR MESSAGE MEANING

Windows Blue Screen with ERROR CODE 714X at line 13322. Google "Error Code 714X at line 13322" and review the results. Sites will display with possible relevant articles posted in a hierarchal search order for that particular search.

Review articles until finding one that helps. If the search doesn't respond with any options, shorten the search. Enter just "Error Code 714X" and see what responses appear.

2. VIRUS REMOVAL

The computer has a popup that says "Your computer is locked and to call Microsoft at this phone number for removal" and the computer isn't usable. Find a different computer and Google and key in the message and check the results. Someone may have posted a removal tool that can be downloaded to remove the virus.

3. HOW TO

Consider adding memory to a computer. First determine the type of memory the system requires and if the system has open memory slots. Search online for the computer make and model and place the word "Memory" in the search. Check the results and order the appropriate memory.

NON COMPUTER PROBLEMS

A search engine isn't limited to troubleshooting computer problems only. Suppose a gas fireplace doesn't ignite. Enter the make and model of the fireplace followed by "Ignition Problem" and check the results.

A riding lawnmower needs a new sparkplug that the local hardware store doesn't stock. Search the Internet and enter in the search engine the make and model of the lawnmower followed by "SPARKPLUG" and check the results. A car dashboard has an error message that isn't listed in the car manual. Google the error message and check the results. Use the Internet to troubleshoot any kind of problem.

DOWNLOAD THE PRODUCT MANUAL

Most companies now place their product manuals online at their web sites. Placing the manual online lessens their cost to bring the product to market. It will take some time and use up ink and paper; however, having a manual to refer to may be of help.

REFINING A SEARCH

If a first search doesn't get an answer to the problem, refine the search. There are different methods to refine a search:

1. Expand the Search
2. Narrow the Search

EXPAND THE SEARCH

Expanding the search is redefining the search from narrow to more general. Let's assume a search for a notebook jack for a specific Hewlett Packard notebook model DV6130US.

If checking Amazon or eBay search for "HPDV6130US jack". If the search returns no results, expand the search by re-entering "DV6000 jack". The search results return results for the entire DV6000 series of jacks instead of just the DV6130.

NARROW THE SEARCH

Narrowing the search redefines the search from a more general to narrow focus. Suppose you started the HP jack search entering "DV6000 jack" and now have hundreds of responses to sort through. Refine and narrow the search by re-entering the specific model – DV6130US.

REVIEW THE POSTS

Knowing how to research the problem doesn't mean that it's easy to find an immediate answer to a problem. Just because someone posts information on the Internet doesn't mean that the Information posted is accurate.

The posts need to be reviewed for accuracy and to make sure the answer works for your particular situation. I spent days researching how to begin numbering pages into a document and must have refined my search at least 25 different times. I watched videos on YouTube. It was not easy; however, I eventually found the correct answer.

Any older people reading this: Remember the days when you had to visit the library and learn to use the card catalog just to find the books necessary to do a research paper?

Research is a lot easier these days online, but you still have to put in the time. There are no shortcuts, unless you are a master of delegation and can find someone to do the research. One difference between a computer technician and non-tech is the amount of time put into researching a program or learning how programs work.

YouTube is a video-sharing website on which users can upload, share and view videos. YouTube can display a wide variety of user-generated video content, including movie clips, TV clips, and music videos, as well as amateur content such as video blogging and short original videos.

YouTube is the ultimate "How To" in training videos. To find out how to do anything computer or non-computer related, search on YouTube. In many cases, YouTube will have a training or How To video on any topic. For example consider watching a YouTube video on replacing a notebook screen if considering tacking that type of job.

REMEMBER THIS

Most of the content on YouTube has been uploaded by individuals, although media corporations including CBS, BBC and Hulu upload and display video as well. Remember that just because someone posted a video on how to do something that the information is correct.

Use a search engine and the Internet to troubleshoot any type of problem.

9. COMMON SENSE REPAIR METHODS

The troubleshooting techniques listed below can be applied to repair any computer problem. Sometimes even the best techs forget to do the simple easy things such as:

KISS

KISS stands for Keep It Simple Stupid. Do not to overthink a problem. Follow these techniques to get a handle on the problem.

1. READ THE SCREEN

The computer does its best to tell you about the problem. If the screen says "memory problem" first reseat or replace memory before checking anything else. "Hard drive imminent failure" means you better get data important off the computer ASAP.

2. TURN POWER OFF AND BACK ON

Turn off power, wait 30 seconds, then turn everything back on again. On occasion a computer gets confused and restarting power corrects whatever was causing the problem.

3. LET WINDOWS DO IT'S THING AND BE PATIENT

Windows has automatic repair features and will attempt to correct itself. Let it run. Be patient with Windows when the repair feature is running or if Windows is installing updates. It could take HOURS. Let it run overnight if necessary, but do not power off the computer.

4. OLDER SYSTEMS STARTUP in SAFE MODE and SELECT "REPAIR MY COMPUTER"

Older versions of Windows (8, 7,) have a Windows Repair feature that may correct the problem. Power on the computer and follow the instructions below:

- Press the F8 key on startup.
- Select SAFE MODE.
- Run REPAIR MY COMPUTER.
- Let the process complete.

5. FOLLOW THE PRINCIPLE OF HALVES

The Principle of Halves is used to describe how to isolate a problem. Become a computer detective and use deductive reasoning to solve the problem. Examples:

DVD NOT READING

If the computer cannot read a DVD, attempt to read the same DVD on a different computer or read multiple DVDs in the same optical drive. If the DVD won't read on the 2nd computer, the problem is most likely with the DVD disc media. The problem has been determined whether the problem lies with the optical drive or the media attempting to be read.

MONITOR NOT WORKING

If a monitor doesn't display a picture, use the same monitor on a different system or setup a different monitor on the same system. Swap out parts to isolate the problem.

With any problem ask the following question:

LTD: WHAT WAS THE LAST THING DONE or CHANGED PRIOR TO THE PROBLEM STARTING?

We call this LTDing the problem. When did the system work last? What changed prior to the problem starting? If it was a program installed, uninstall it. If a printer was installed, disconnect it first and then uninstall the printer software. Try different mice, keyboards, and monitors; remove software programs one at a time at test to see if the problem was corrected after each change. One doesn't have to be a computer genius, just change one thing at a time and write down what was swapped.

Was a new program installed? Was a device driver updated? Was Windows updated? Was a mail attachment opened? Was anyone on a social networking site? Something triggered the problem and work backward starting with the last change prior to first experiencing the problem.

5. CHECK ONLINE

Check the FAQs (Frequently Asked Questions) at the hardware or software vendor's website. Microsoft has a wealth of information and possible solutions to problems and solutions at support.microsoft.com.

6. CHECK THE MANUAL AND HELP ME FILES

The problem may be described in the manual or in a READ ME FILE on the computer.

7. CHECK WITH YOUR GURU

Your guru is anyone that knows more about computers than you. It could be a family member, relative, or the IT guy at work.

8. CHECK WITH THE LOCAL COMPUTER REPAIR CENTER

This option was listed last because if the computer isn't under warranty the out-of-warranty help may not be free. A major reason to purchase from a local computer store is to build a relationship with the person selling the system. The guy working at that large computer chain store probably won't be there within a year

Use common sense and the Principle of Halves.

10. BACKUP YOUR DATA

AFTER CRUCIAL INFORMATION WAS INADVERTENTLY ERASED, EXPERTS WERE CALLED IN TO PERFORM DATA RECOVERY

BACKUP
BACKUP
BACKUP

If you don't remember anything from this book,

REMEMBER THIS

CONSISTENTLY BACKUP the USERS or MY DOCUMENTS folder and all important files off the computer.

This chapter is the most important chapter in this book. Backing up important data off the computer is the single most important PC habit to follow.

REMEMBER THIS

There isn't any serious computer problem IF important data is backed up.

BACKUP METHODS

There are two main methods to back up important files. Both methods include saving important data at some location off the computer. Remember that at some point in time that computer will not be usable, which means the data will not be accessible until the computer is fixed. Back up data to either of the following places:

1. External device or media, such as a flash drive, hard drive or other type of media.
2. Backing up on the Internet to "The Cloud".

EXTERNAL BACKUP DEVICES

USB FLASH DRIVE

A flash drive is a small device that is used for file storage. A flash drive is a portable storage method similar to a CD or a floppy disk. Flash drives are made in different storage capacity sizes, similar to hard drives. A flash drive connects to any computer USB port.

Windows will recognize the flash drive as a new storage drive letter (usually E, F, or G). Files can be transferred from the computer hard drive to the flash drive. Flash drives are inexpensive and good for copying smaller amounts of information.

USB EXTERNAL HARD DRIVE

USB External Hard Drives work like USB flash drives. They connect to any USB port and can be used to copy and store data. The only difference is that a USB hard drive has a greater storage capacity.

External hard drives are a better option to backup video files or anything that takes up large amounts of storage space. Windows will designate a specific letter for the hard drive or any external storage device as it would with a flash drive or any external storage device.

HOW MUCH STORAGE SPACE IS REQUIRED FOR A BACKUP?

The storage size of the folder includes all documents, pictures and music. Usually documents take up the least amount of space, videos files are the largest files and music and photos are somewhere in between.

Typically the USERS or MY DOCUMENTS folder with only Word and Excel files and a few hundred photos shouldn't take up more than 10 gigabytes of storage space. Add many photos videos and music and the space requirements could raise up to 100 gigabytes of space or more.

FILE TYPE	STORAGE SPACE NEEDED
Word and Excel Documents	Up to 5 Gigabytes
Photos	Up to 100 Gigabytes
Music	Up to 100 Gigabytes
Video	Up to 500 Gigabytes

HOW TO DETERMINE DATA STORAGE REQUIREMENTS

Find the USERS folder on the C drive. The USERS folder will contain all files from all Users on the computer, including documents on the desktop.

- Find the USERS Folder.
- Right Click on the Folder.
- Left Click on PROPERTIES.

Any files and folders placed on the desktop should be automatically backed up if the entire MY DOCUMENTS Folder is saved.

Backing up the USERS FOLDER backs up all files, photos and music from all USERS UNLESS the user saved the files in a different location. Saving the MY DOCUMENTS folder may not automatically backup files in programs like QuickBooks and TurboTax. Those files are saved in separate folders.

Programs like QuickBooks and TurboTax need to have their data saved within their program. Most application programs have a BACKUP option under the FILE Menu at the top left in their program main menu.

To backup QuickBooks files:

- Open the QuickBooks program
- Within the QuickBooks program, SELECT FILE and BACKUP.
- Select the external device to save to.

The same process should be followed to backup data from any non-Windows program.

1. Within the program, select FILE and SAVE AS.
2. Backup the data to the external hard drive or flash drive.

BACKUP CONSTANTLY

Get in the habit of backing up data every 5 minutes to external storage. If power is lost, the more data that's backed up, the less you have to re-enter or re-create.

HOW TO SETUP AN AUTOMATIC BACKUP

Automatic backup can be setup in Windows. To setup an automatic backup in Windows using an external device:

1. Open CONTROL PANEL / SYSTEM / BACKUP AND RESTORE
2. Click on the SET UP BACKUP at top right corner.
3. Select the External backup drive to back up to and check NEXT.
4. Select what to backup. Make sure to include ALL USER FOLDERS.
5. Select the BACKUP SCHEDULE, save settings and Exit.

HOW TO BACKUP EXTERNALLY

TO A FLASH OR EXTERNAL DRIVE

1. Open MY PC and review the drive letters assigned by Windows.

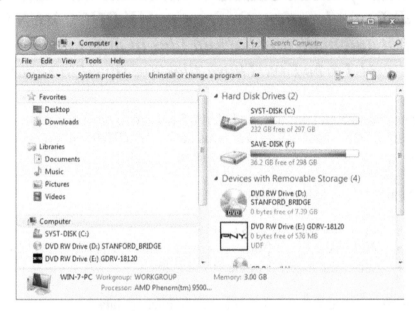

The system disk (C) should be the location of the Windows operating system. Windows assigns a letter designation to each alternate storage device area – possibly D or E or E and F for the optical drive(s). Windows will automatically assign letters for other temporary storage devices, such as a camera or phone.

2. Insert the flash drive into any USB port and continue to review the list. A new letter will appear within a minute. That is the letter Windows assigned to the external flash drive.

3. Check that the folder to backup isn't larger than the available space on the flash drive. If copying an entire folder, such as a MY DOCUMENTS folder, right click on the folder and select PROPERTIES. Check the amount of available space on the flash drive by right clicking on the flash drive icon and selecting PROPERTIES and compare the file size against the amount of free space left on the external backup device.

4. Right click on the USERS Folder / Select SEND TO/ Select the drive letter that represents the flash drive.

It's important to alternate backup devices. Flash drives can fail or get lost. Hard drives crash. Things break. My QuickBooks is backed up on two computers and three separate flash drives at two separate locations. If something catastrophic happened at one location, my QuickBooks data is still recoverable. Make sure to alternate data backups to different devices or locations.

My less important files and documents are only stored on two separate flash drives. The point is backing up data should be as much a part of your computing routine as turning the computer on and off. Any lost data due to not backing up is the fault of the user. There is no one else to blame.

BACKING UP TO THE CLOUD

Storing data in the Cloud refers to electronically backing up and storing files online using the Internet instead of on the computer hard drive or external backup drive.

Select sites allow a free backup for a very limited amount of data. Free storage accounts usually allow up to five gigabytes of data storage prior to charging.

Online backup services will backup data files automatically, so data will still get saved. Alternative backup sites include Box.net, Dropbox, Google Docs and SkyDrive by Microsoft. Review each to see which online service best fits your requirements and budget.

ONLINE CLOUD ADVANTAGES

The main advantage of backing up online is that the data is placed at a separate location. Suppose the home or office burned down? Maybe the computer was stolen or destroyed by a fire. Both the data and backup are lost. Data saved online can be accessed from a separate location and computer if the account login information is accessible.

Another cloud advantage is that most online backup services can be automatically setup to backup data without user intervention, unlike backing up externally. A cloud backup might be a better option for a person that "will get to it later."

ONLINE CLOUD DISADVANTAGES

1. TRUST AND CONTROL

The main disadvantage of a cloud backup is lack of control over the data. Online data can be stolen by hackers or a cloud company employee. If the data storage site or Internet provider is down, the online backup will not be available.

Assume any information placed on the web will be seen by someone besides the intended party. If the data is of a very private nature, consider not saving it online. Take that approach with any online correspondence including emails and attachments.

2. ACCESS AND SPEED

At times Internet access may not be an option. Data saved in the Cloud cannot be retrieved without Internet access. Retrieving saved data from the web may take longer than expected.

Using an online backup site is like placing a claim with an insurance company. The data will probably be recovered; however, the time frame may not be to your liking.

Most cloud applications don't have the functionality or flexibility of local desktop applications. Local desktop applications will work faster than comparable cloud applications. Don't throw out all that desktop software just yet.

3. WHO IS WATCHING AND READING?

Every company states that they protect your information and privacy; however, who knows what's done with information once it's uploaded?

Ask yourself who would be harmed if someone else gained access to your data. Online data files posted to the Internet should NEVER contain social security numbers or personal financial information.

ASK THESE QUESTIONS PRIOR TO STORING DATA ONLINE.

1. Can I be hurt personally if the wrong person gained access to this information?
2. Can I be hurt or will it bother me if this information remains on the web permanently?

Reconsider posting data online if the answer is YES to either question.

STORE RECOVERY MEDIA AND KEYCODES IN A SAFE PLACE

Keep program Media flash drives, CDs or DVDs in a safe place. The CDs or DVDs will be necessary to re-install the programs. Keep all information and Key code with the program CDs.

The key code is the registration number needed during the installation. The key code communicates to the software company that the program being installed and activated is a legal licensed copy.

Copy the license key code and store it separately, in case the key code on the unit or software becomes unreadable or lost. If that key code gets lost, the software will have to be repurchased.

Do not lose the registration key code to any program. A software company is not going to provide a second registration key code free of charge, no matter the reason or excuse. My key codes are kept in a safer location than my wallet. The program will have to be re-purchased if a key code is misplaced or stolen.

Backup your data. Keep multiple backups at different locations.

11. HOW TO REPAIR MOST SOFTWARE PROBLEMS

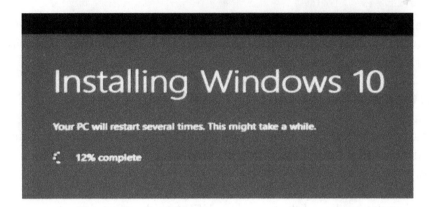

When customers are presented with options that include either a Windows re-installation or a less invasive Windows repair option, most people rather have us attempt the less invasive repair.

People prefer to have their computer working better with less aggravation to deal with than having to spend additional time starting over from scratch and re-installing programs. There are advantages and disadvantages to re-installing Windows.

Windows Re-installation Advantages

1. ULTIMATE TEST FOR HARDWARE versus SOFTWARE PROBLEM

Sometimes a hardware problem won't surface until Windows is re-installed. Suppose the computer has really slowed up. If Windows is re-installed and the computer is still running slowly, that's an indication that the hard drive may be failing. The computer now runs properly, the system just had corrupted Windows and is now and running at 100% again.

2. THE SOFTWARE PROBLEM WILL BE CORRECTED

Whatever the software problem – virus, spyware, malware, registry issue, program or driver conflict or just plain corrupted Windows should be corrected with a Windows re-installation. Most software problems should be corrected if the hard drive is formatted and a fresh installation of Windows is installed.

A less invasive repair such as a virus and spyware removal or Windows repair may not correct the problem as well or as long as a full Windows re-installation.

3. THE COMPUTER SHOULD WORK BETTER

An added benefit of re-installing Windows is the computer will work faster. The drive formatting and Windows re-installation also removed all the junk programs, downloads and files that have built up on computer. A Windows re-installation provides the added benefit of giving the computer an optimization.

4. NOW DEALING WITH A CERTAINTY

If the computer still has issues after a fresh Windows re-installation the problem is probably hardware and the computer can be moved forward with a hardware repair.

The Disadvantages of Re-installing Windows:

1. LOSS OF PROGRAMS

A Windows re-installation will remove any programs that were installed separately from Windows. Microsoft Office, Turbo Tax, QuickBooks, or any other program that was installed separate from the Windows operating system.

When a user has legal copies of each program and have the installation download or DVDs safely stored, re-installing programs such as Microsoft Office or Anti-Virus software shouldn't be a problem. Re-installing any freeware programs should not be a problem. Only software that was installed on the computer illegally may be a problem re-installing.

ILLEGAL SOFTWARE

Everyone has the friend or relative that loves to "help out" by installing programs on a computer that weren't legally purchased. One could ask that person if they can re-install the software; however, the odds are less that the software will re-activate a second time. That person may not be available to assist you in the future. Purchase software or use free software and expect to have less trouble re-installing programs in the future.

2. RE-INSTALLING WINDOWS TAKES TIME

Re-installing Windows and programs can take time. The basic re-installation is then followed by multiple sets of updates that can take hours or even days.

Device drivers have to be updated followed by re-installing all the non-Windows programs. The computer can be used while it is updating. How much time is wasted running a slower computer or a computer that continually freezes or blue screens? You can spend hours running virus and spyware removal programs and still end up having to re-install Windows.

3. IMPORTANT FILES OR DATA WILL BE LOST

Remember one of the golden rules is to BACKUP YOUR DATA. This argument has no merit if the data is safely backed up off the computer.

MAKE A BOOTABLE REPAIR / RECOVERY USB OR DVD MEDIA

A Windows Repair or Recovery USB or DVD is a very useful item to have. The Repair media can be used if Windows doesn't start. Place the Recovery USB drive or DVD in the system and restart the computer. Change the boot order so that the computer will boot to the recovery media.

The Repair / Recovery media will provide options to either start or repair the system. To make a recovery media, select RECOVERY and follow the prompts to MAKE RECOVERY MEDIA.

A complete Windows re-installation should correct any software problem.

12. HOW TO RE-INSTALL WINDOWS

If ten people were randomly on the street and asked if they knew how to re-install Windows how many people would answer yes? My guess is possibly two of ten people can re-install their Windows.

Computers today are easier to re-install Windows. Once Windows is learned to be re-installed, one can perform most software repairs almost as well as any technician and save money in the process.

WHAT IS WINDOWS CORRUPTION AND WHAT CAUSES IT?

Windows corruption is when Windows doesn't work right. Windows gets wacky for lack of a better word. Windows corruption symptoms are discussed later.

Windows corruption can be caused by any number of things – viruses, spyware, malware, device driver updates, Windows updates, shutting the computer down improperly, power outages, hardware failure, an installed program that Windows doesn't like or any combination of these causes.

Windows doesn't need a considerable amount of outside help to get corrupted. Even something as non-threatening as a Windows update could cause a problem. When people ask what caused Windows to get corrupted, I can give an educated guess, but am never 100% positive. It's similar to asking the car mechanic where the tire picked up the nail that he's removing.

HOW TO KNOW A WINDOWS RE-INTALLATION IS NECESSARY

If the following fixes have been tried and the computer still isn't working properly, the system probably needs a Windows re-installation.

1. Running virus, spyware and malware removal programs.
2. Tried a restore point repair (discussed later).
3. Turned off all invasive programs running.
4. The system runs very slow and blue screen error messages.
5. The system doesn't start in Safe Mode
6. All important data is backed up.

WINDOWS REPAIR

Windows has a set of ADVANCED OPTIONS to help correct Windows problems without having to perform a complete Windows Re-installation. The REPAIR option in Windows can correct Windows problems without having to completely re-install Windows.

A Windows Repair runs when Windows tries to correct itself. The latest versions of Windows should automatically correct itself. Let Windows complete the process, do not stop it. Sometimes the Repair process will work.

A Windows Repair may automatically run without the user having to do anything. Do not stop or break a Windows repair once it begins. Let the Repair run to its completion. It could take half a day to complete.

RESTORE POINT RECOVERY

System Restore will take the computer back in time to an earlier working state, without affecting any files or documents. Windows automatically saves Restore Point backups when something significant happens, such as installing a Windows Update or a new application. A user can make Restore Point backups any time.

The concept behind the Restore Point is that if something goes wrong, the user can return to the last Restore Point (or an even earlier one) to turn back and get the computer working correctly again. A Restore Point recovery only works if the user has made a restore point backup so the recovery can be run.

TO CREATE A RESTORE POINT·

1. Select Control Panel / Recovery / Configure System Restore.
2. Make sure the restore point option is turned on the C DRIVE to make a backup. Allocate at least 10-20% for a storage area to save a backup.
3. Select CREATE
4. Name the Restore Point for later reference and click OK.

RESTORE A WINDOWS COMPUTER USING A RESTORE POINT

1. Select Control Panel / Recovery / Open SYSTEM RESTORE
2. Select the option to View other restore points
3. Select the created restore point or the restore point at the top of the list (most recent).

NOTE: Multiple restore points are listed chronologically. The most recent restore point will be listed at the top. Try the top restore point first and work your way down the list.

IF THE RESTORE POINT DOESN' T WORK

Boot up into Windows 10 Safe mode by restarting the computer hand holding down the SHIFT KEY (Older Windows hold down the F8 key). Running the computer in SAFE MODE eliminates the possibility of other programs and drivers causing a problem. If the Restore Point recovery option doesn't work, move on to the RESET Options.

RESET THE SYSTEM WITHOUT SAVING DATA

A Windows 10 System Reset without saving files re-installs Windows and removes all data. All photos, documents and music are removed. Most non-Windows programs are removed.

A SYSTEM RESET CAN BE PERFORMED EITHER SAVING OR NOT SAVING DATA. NOT SAVING DATA REMOVES ALL DOCUMENTS, MUSIC AND PHOTOS.

A system reset removing all files should correct any software problem, and will remove all files and programs installed on the computer, including MICROSOFT OFFICE. Everything on the computer is taken back in time to the condition when the computer was originally purchased:

When we discuss a Windows re-load with a customer, we explain that when they get their computer back, Microsoft Office will not be installed. Microsoft Office is a productivity suite that consist of the Microsoft Word word-processing and Microsoft Excel spreadsheet programs.

These programs are not part of or contained within Windows. Microsoft Office is a separate program that has its own license and DVD or download. When we re-install a manufacturer version of Windows, what gets re-installed is a Trial version of Microsoft Office that will shut down within 30 days.

WINDOWS RESET THE SYSTEM SAVING DATA

Windows 10 and future versions have what is called a RESET option within RECOVERY. A Windows RESET will re-install Windows.

A Windows system reset can be performed SAVING FILES. This is a less invasive option and should be tried first especially if the data hasn't been backed up for some time. THIS OPTION WILL STILL REMOVE THE NON-WINDOWS PROGRAMS. Microsoft Office and other programs will still have to be re-installed.

The data being saved are all USER folders and files. Windows will save the documents, music and photos, but again non-Windows programs like Microsoft Office, Adobe Photoshop and TurboTax will have to be re-installed.

WINDOWS RE-INSTALLATION

Prior to performing a full Windows Reset or Reload:

1. TAKE INVENTORY

Is the recovery media available to re-install programs? Will a Windows key code for re-activation be necessary and available? The key codes will be necessary to re-activate the program on the Internet. Look into all these potential issues prior to starting a Windows reload. If the computer had Windows 10 originally installed, Windows 10 should automatically re-activate once re-installed and back online.

2. BACKUP

Backup all important files. Copy the entire USERS folder and any non-Windows data such as QuickBooks, Adobe Photoshop, Quicken and any other important files.

HOW TO RE-INSTALL WINDOWS

KEYSTROKE RECOVERY

Today's computers have a single keystroke recovery system that permits the user to re-install Windows with the touch of one key or at least get into the computer Recovery console. Lenovo has their one touch recovery which can be a keystroke or a pin hole on the side of the unit. HP usually gets into recovery mode by pressing the ESC or F11 key.

To find what keystroke works with your computer, check the computer manufacturer website or GOOGLE the make and model computer and use the words "Windows Recovery" or "Windows Re-installation".

OTHER KEYSTROKE WINDOWS RECOVERY OPTIONS

- F10, F11 or F12 for most computers or notebooks.
- F4 - F6 for netbooks.
- Older computers press the F8 key on startup / Select REPAIR MY COMPUTER / Select IMAGE RECOVERY.

RECOVERY MEDIA

On occasion computers may ship with Windows OS recovery DVDs or give the buyer the capability to create a backup set of recovery media. Make a backup set of DVDs. Microsoft allow allows downloads of their operating systems onto bootable USB drives.

A system should allow the making of a bootable backup recovery onto a flash drive. A 16 gig size flash drive should be large enough to copy a Windows image backup.

RE-INSTALLING WINDOWS USING RECOVERY MEDIA

1. First place the USB drive in the USB port or a Windows DVD into the DVD drive and restart the computer.
2. Press the F12 Key to access the BOOT ORDER.
3. Select either the Flash Drive or Recovery DVD as the bootable media.
4. When the prompt appears to "Press any Key to boot" quickly press any key to make Windows load from the installation media.

IF THE RELOAD PROCESS DOESN'T START FROM THE DVD

If the installation process isn't starting, it's possible that the computer start-up sequence is set to first search the hard drive for a bootable operating system to start and the F12 selection isn't overriding the start-up order choices.

CHANGE THE START-UP OR BOOT SEQUENCE IN THE BIOS

To change the startup sequence in the Setup utility so the computer will automatically look to load from a Windows bootable media on startup:

1. Enter SETUP on system start-up (Press theF1, F2, DELETE key or the key sequence gets the system into system startup).
2. Find the BOOT SEQUENCE OR STARTUP OPTION.
3. Change the boot selection order and SAVE THE CHANGES.

UEFI VERSUS LEGACY BOOT OPTIONS

BIOS and UEFI are two firmware interfaces stored in a computer system BIOS for computers. The UEFI is the newer system configuration and LEGACY is the older BIOS version.

Some older computers need Windows to be re-installed using the Legacy version of the system setup. If Windows will not re-install onto the computer, re-install Windows using the LEGACY Bios Setup option under the system boot up options.

RE-INSTALL WINDOWS FROM A MANUFACTURER RECOVERY PARTITION

This is a screen from a computer manufacturer's recovery partition program. Each system may have a different look and different options; however, the recovery partition purpose for every computer serves the same function - to re-install Windows back to the condition when the system was first purchased.

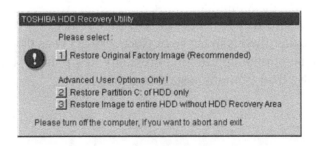

DISADVANTAGES

The problem with a manufacturer partition recovery is that older software is restored back onto the system. After a manufacturer Windows recovery finishes, the first order of business is to get Windows updates. Manufacturer hardware device drivers should be updated.

A manufacturer partition recovery will only replace additional programs that came with the system. Any software installed by the user after receiving the system typically will be lost on the manufacturer Windows installation.

WHAT TO DO IF WINDOWS DOESN'T RE-INSTALL

Be aware that a partition recovery can get deleted or just be corrupted. If that occurs, get manufacturer recovery media or take the computer to a repair center.

If all possible keystroke combinations don't work and cannot the Windows re-installation won't begin:

1. Read the screen when turning on the computer. The manufacturer should list the specific key sequence to press to begin the recovery process; however, the information doesn't remain on the screen very long.
2. Search how to re-install Windows for the system online by Googling the make and model of the computer followed by "RECOVERY" or "RESTORE". Information on how to re-install the computer online.
3. Check the manufacturer's website for directions.
4. Contact the store where the computer was purchased.
5. Contact the manufacturer to purchase Recovery Media.

WINDOWS LICENSING

Large computer manufacturers like Dell, HP and Acer have their own agreements with Microsoft regarding Windows licensing for their computers. Most Windows based computers should have a Windows license on the side or bottom of the computer. That license number may be required to re-activate the computer with Microsoft after Windows is re-installed.

In most cases, Windows will automatically reactivate once the computer is back on the internet because Microsoft determined online that particular computer had a legal licensed copy of Windows.

INSTALLING WINDOWS

Once Windows begin re-installing, the INITIAL process can take anywhere up to an hour. The system may restart multiple times. Re-installing from an image takes very little time, while installing from Windows recovery media can take hours.

FINAL WINDOWS SETUP

Once Windows files compete copying from the image, flash drive or DVDs, Windows will ask a series of 10-15 questions.

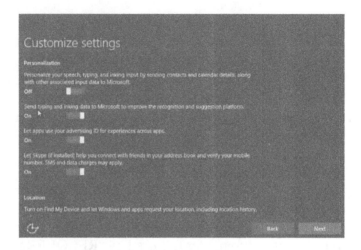

BE ADVISED

Microsoft is in the information collection business. Read the questions carefully. Any YES answer is providing some type of information to Microsoft. Answer NO to most Microsoft questions from accessing hotspots to sending diagnostic information.

GET WINDOWS UPDATES

Windows Update is a service provided by Microsoft that provides software updates for Windows. Newer versions of Windows will automatically check and download updates. The user has the option to control the update process. Once Windows is re-installed, manually check for updates:

- Select PC SETTINGS
- Select SECURITY AND UPDATES
- Manually select CHECK FOR UPDATES

Windows will search for updates on all Microsoft software including Defender Anti-Virus and Microsoft Office. It is a good idea to stay current with Windows updates. It's a good idea to at least once a month to manually check for Windows updates, just to make sure the system is receiving them.

If the system gets behind with Windows updates, it may take a long time to complete updates to get current. A computer will restart multiple times to complete all Windows updates.

EXPRESS VERSUS CUSTOM UPDATES

Express Updates is easier; however, Custom Updates allows the user to pick and choose specific Windows updates to install or not install. To have updates only update the Microsoft software without updating hardware devices, select Custom updates.

Custom updates permit a user to not install a particular update that may be a known problem with the computer. Custom updates are for the advanced user.

DO NOT INTERRUPT THE UPDATE PROCESS ONCE STARTED

Windows updates can take hours to over a day to complete. Let the Windows update process complete once it begins. Breaking the update process can corrupt Windows. Do not interrupt the configuration process when the computer restarts.

UPDATE DEVICE DRIVERS

Windows updates in many cases will update the hardware device drivers; however, it is a good idea to check for device driver updates. It may take 10-20 minutes to check for device drivers. To individually check for device drivers, follow the following steps:

- Enter CONTROL PANEL
- Select DEVICE DRIVERS
- Right click on each device driver
- Select UPDATE DRIVER

Windows will automatically search the internet for the latest driver for that device, then download and install it. Select each device. Minimally, check for COMPUTER, DISPLAY and NETWORK drivers.

There are third party free device driver programs available, however in most cases these programs will also place junk on the computer and in most cases should be avoided.

HOW TO AUTOMATICALLY UPDATE ALL DRIVERS

Follow the steps listed below to automatically update all device drivers at once.

- Enter CONTROL PANEL
- Select DEVICES AND PRINTERS
- Right-click the name of the computer, and Select DEVICE INSTALLATION
- Select YES, do this automatically (recommended), and then click Save changes.

WHAT IF THE SYSTEM CANNOT GET ON THE INTERNET FOR UPDATES?

This can happen. The usual reason is that the network device drivers were not re-installed The Internet access problem must be solved before going ahead. Sometimes a Windows re-installation did not re-install the network driver.

Hopefully the manufacturer re-installation will install the device drivers; however, that doesn't always happen. An inexpensive fix for this type of problem is a USB network adapter. A USB network adapter is an ethernet adapter that will connect to a USB port on the computer and the other end will connect to a network cable. The adapter should include a device driver. Install the driver and use it to get on the Internet. These devices can be purchased wirelessly. A USB network adapter should cost about $25.

RE-INSTALL APPLICATION PROGRAMS

Once Windows and the drivers are installed and updated, application programs need to be re-installed. Install the programs and check for program updates. Each program may need to be re-activated online.

Assuming the programs were legally purchased, re-install the programs over the Internet or use the original program installation media. Once completed, check each program for program updates over the internet.

DATA RESTORE

Any saved data needs to be restored back onto the computer and into the application programs. Insert the backup device with the backed up data. Run a restore from each program and point to the data.

To restore QuickBooks data, the RESTORE option must be run from the QuickBooks program. Point the program to where the backup data is located.

If the QuickBooks QDATA backup file is located on an external flash drive, the restore must point to the flash drive (E, F, G or whatever letter the flash drive is represented by in Windows), the QuickBooks folder and the specific file. Any saved documents and photos can be placed into the USERS folder on the new system.

Re-installing Windows may seem like a lot of work; however, the system should work properly and faster – at least for a while.

WINDOWS IMAGE CREATION

A user may want to create an entire image backup of the computer hard drive for restoration purposes. This process should work in older versions of Windows as well as the most current version.

1. Select CONTROL PANEL / FILE HISTORY.
2. Select SYSTEM IMAGE BACKUP
3. The System Image Backup utility will open.
4. Pick a place to save a system image backup (on a hard disk, on one or more DVDs, or on a network location), and click Next. Confirm the settings and click START BACKUP. Make sure to have enough free backup space to create the backup. An external hard drive is recommended for this process.

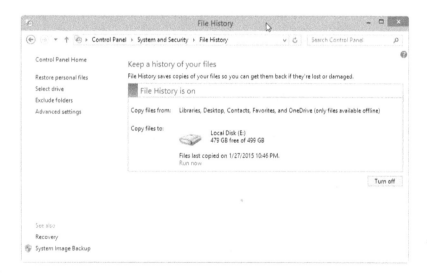

The computer screens show where to make a complete system image backup. Check CONTROL PANEL or PC SETTINGS and RECOVERY or FILE BACKUP to access these screens.

RESTORE FROM A SYSTEM BACKUP

1. Select the SETTINGS menu / Select UPDATE & RECOVERY.
2. Select the ADVANCED STARTUP section / Click RESTART NOW.
3. When the PC restarts, select TROUBLESHOOT, ADVANCED OPTIONS / SYSTEM IMAGE RECOVERY.

MORE RECOVERY OPTIONS

Press F11 or other Function Key when powering on. Booting off an install disk and hitting NEXT / REPAIR may work. The following screen should appear:

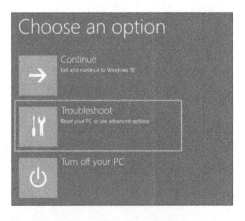

Select TROUBLESHOOT / ADVANCED OPTIONS

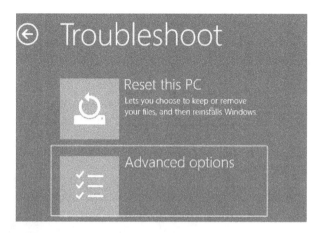

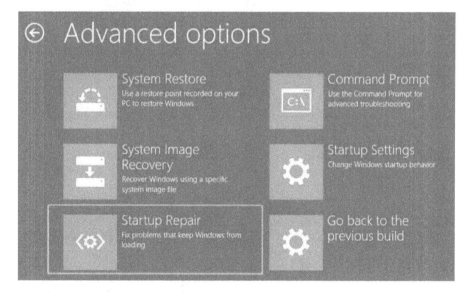

Select STARTUP REPAIR.

Windows can take a few minutes to hours to attempt to fix the problem. Let the repair complete. Sometimes the repair may work; however, in most cases it will not.

If the Startup Repair does not work, repair the system using a WINDOWS RESTORE. To run System Restore, boot into the same screen above and select SYSTEM RESTORE. There are other more advanced correction methods, but at this point if the computer will not work, **RE-INSTALL WINDOWS.**

RE-INSTALL WINDOWS FROM THE MICRSOFT SITE

Microsoft provides access to downloading Windows re-installation files from Microsoft's website. Find WINDOWS DOWNLOADS on the Microsoft website. The current program to accept is the MEDIA CREATION TOOL, but it could be different by the time you read this.

Select "CREATE INSTALLATION MEDIA FOR ANOTHER PC". Windows can be copied to a USB flash drive or make an ISO file.

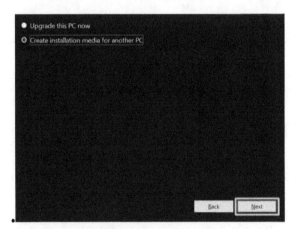

At this point GOOGLE how to do this because whatever is written here will be slightly altered. Use Google and search "Windows creator's update download".

OLDER SYSTEMS

With older version of Windows, the SAFE MODE option may be available. To access older Windows SAFE MODE, press the F8 KEY when starting the computer.

WINDOWS SAFE MODE OPTIONS

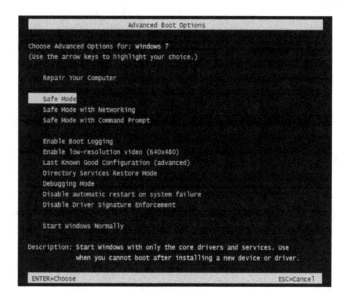

RUNNING WINDOWS REPAIR IN SAFE MODE

This screen is shown when pressing the F8 key on startup on an older Windows 8 or older system. Select this option if operating Windows 8 or older.

Windows may automatically repair the computer without having to do a reload. At times running the REPAIR YOUR COMPUTER may automatically correct the problem. Computer manufacturers provide a menu under this option that will enable a user to perform a complete Windows re-installation. Enter this screen on the computer to check the options.

SAFE MODE

Safe Mode starts Windows without installing hardware device drivers or any other non-Windows programs. Safe Mode is a stripped down version of Windows without loading programs on startup.

SAFE MODE WITH NETWORKING

SAFE MODE WITH NETWORKING is similar to SAFE MODE; however, network drivers are installed on the system. The computer may be able to access the Internet; however, the computer shouldn't be permanently used in Safe Mode.

LAST KNOWN GOOD CONFIGURATION

This is an abbreviated Restore Point where the computer will be taken back in time to the last known working configuration. This option can be tried if Windows isn't working properly.

WHAT'S THE BEST OPTION - REPAIR, RELOAD OR RESTORE POINTS?

It depends. If pressed for time, run the Restore Point fix first. The repair may or may not fix the problem and will take a while to run. The Restore Point has a greater chance of fixing the problem. Even if the Restore Point works, the system still must be checked for viruses and spyware. Going back to a restore point doesn't mean that whatever originally caused the problem is no longer going to affect the computer.

If the data and programs are important, run the restore points first, repair second and reload as a last result. If the computer doesn't boot into Windows, the Repair has to be attempted first.

If losing the data and programs isn't an issue, go ahead and re-install Windows. A Windows reload will guarantee that the software problem will be corrected and the computer will work better as a second benefit. Time won't be wasted attempting a Repair or Restore Point that may not repair the problem.

RESET VERSUS COMPLETE RE-INSTALLATION

A Windows RESET is done using the Windows files on the computer while a complete Windows RE-INSTALLATION is performed using software either from an external bootable device or the Microsoft website.

If time isn't an issue, select RESET SAVING DATA first. If that doesn't work, try RESET NOT SAVING DATA next. If neither reset process works, next try re-installing Windows using software from either a DVD, USB flash drive or the Microsoft Website.

Sometimes the software being used the reset a computer is corrupted. We've found over the years that some manufacturer software recovery partitions sometimes don't correctly re-install Windows. In that case separate media recovery must be used.

WINDOWS WON'T ACTIVATE AFTER A RE-INSTALLATION

Windows should activate once re-installed. Check under CONTROL PANEL / SYSTEM to verify activation.

If Windows doesn't activate, check to make sure that the correct version of Windows was re-installed back onto the computer. If the computer had the HOME version of Windows originally and PROFESSIONAL was re-installed Windows will not activate.

Attempt to re-activate Windows online by trying the activation process and re-keying the product key code on the system. If that doesn't work, Microsoft may have to be called on the phone to get activated over the phone.

Learn how to re-install Windows to avoid paying for computer service.

13. ACTIVATION & REGISTRATION

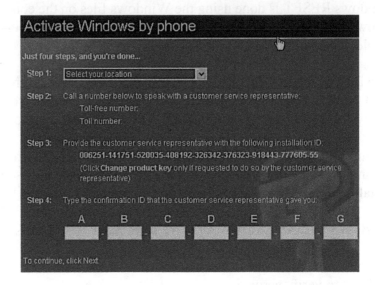

Activation is a process when a newly installed program on a system is recognized by the program's company online as being a legal version of the product and gives the installer the right to use it. The software company has "blessed" you as a valid user for using that particular program. The company verifies either through an online or phone process that the program being installed is a legal licensed version of their software.

WHY PROGRAMS NEED TO BE ACTIVATED

Software companies require activation on most programs due to the rampant illegal copying and distribution of software. Software pirating is a world-wide problem and is difficult to control. When a program is illegally copied, the software creator receives no compensation of any type. Software pirates purchase illegal copies of Microsoft Windows and Office and distribute the programs.

Software piracy has reached new heights over the Internet. Hackers develop programs that can install and activate various programs. Key codes for products are placed online for people to download and get programs activated. Programs are placed online for download and distribution.

Most programs once installed on the computer prompt to activate automatically once online. The program will prompt "Do you want to activate your copy?" Select "Yes" the program should activate over the Internet.

IS ACTIVATION NECESSARY?

Most programs allow use of their software for a period of time without activation. Many programs run for 30 days then shut down if they aren't activated.

PHONE ACTIVATION

If the program won't activate online call the Software Company on the phone to get an activation code. Have the following ready if calling on the phone to activate software:

1. The Activation Window open and be online with the computer.
2. The key code.
3. A purchase receipt or email if the program was a download purchase.
4. A pencil and paper.

The person on the phone may ask questions like "why are you installing this software?" or "is this software installed on any other computer?" Answer each question honestly and only answer the question asked. Do not volunteer any additional information. Pretend you're talking to the IRS.

WINDOWS ACTIVATION

Microsoft requires that Windows needs to be re-activated whenever a Windows repair or reload is performed. Activation can be done automatically when the computer is back online.

If the computer has Windows 10 or later version of and needs to be re-installed because of a hard drive or other hardware failure, Windows should automatically re-activate once the computer is back on the internet.

PROGRAM KEYCODE

A key code is a specific series of letters and numbers that must be entered when installing the program.

When the program gains access to the Internet, that series of letters and numbers is transmitted to the vendor. The vendor then "activates" the computer for use. The activation is a validation process.

WHEN TO ACTIVATE

Activate Windows or any program that requires activation as soon as possible. Activate Windows prior to downloading all Windows updates. Determine as soon as possible if activating Windows is going to be a problem.

We mentioned earlier that in many cases if the computer was operating under Windows 10 or later, the system should automatically re-activate once the computer is back on the internet as long as the system was reload with the same version of Windows.

REASONS WHY SOFTWARE WON'T ACTIVATE

1. ILLEGAL OR INVALID COPY

The license on a computer is for that particular version of Windows for that single system only. That computer will not work with a different version of Windows without purchasing a full or upgrade version.

For example, if the system is licensed and using Windows 8, the user would have to purchase either an upgrade or full version of Windows 10. Microsoft offered free Windows 10 upgrades for a while, however, that program ended. Every legal copy of Windows must have a key code for the upgraded software to be used for activation.

Say no to the friend, neighbor or co-worker that offers to install a different version of Windows on your system. Windows probably won't activate or work.

2. TOO MANY HARDWARE CHANGES

Too many hardware changes were made to the computer. Windows sees the computer as a different system than what the computer was originally licensed and activated. Suppose the system took a power surge and the motherboard and hard drive had to be replaced. When attempting to get a computer activated, the Microsoft activation server may see the original key code attempting to activate a different computer. You may need to get on the phone with Microsoft and explain the situation to get the system re-activated.

3. KEYCODE USED TOO MANY TIMES

The Microsoft activation server has determined that the key code on the system has been activated too many times. This can occur with older systems. A phone call to Microsoft may be necessary to get the problem corrected.

4. MICROSOFT ACTIVATION SERVER HAS A PROBLEM

The Microsoft activation server can get overloaded. Every PC manufacturer computer should have a Windows license. Call Microsoft to get the problem solved.

5. PHONE ACTIVATION

Activating a copy of Windows isn't as painful as it used to be. Microsoft has an automated phone service for activation. One can search online for "Microsoft activation phone number" if the number is not available.

Microsoft will ask a series of questions, one of which will be on how many times or how many computers is this software installed? The answer should be ONE.

UPDATE ADVANTAGES

The main advantage to activate a program is to get program updates. The program updates alone should be reason to activate.

REGISTRATION

Companies want users to register their software products so they have access to a customer's information for resale or to market software or hardware upgrades or other products at a later date. Sometimes registering software is necessary as part of the activation process to use the software.

WHY REGISTER A PRODUCT?

Yes, if the registration is required to receive technical support, updates and warranty coverage. Registering a product is a win-win for both the user and the company. The company gets information on a customer and the customer is able to get support from the user and the company.

WHY PEOPLE DO NOT REGISTER

A person won't register if they don't really care about updates and don't want to receive solicitations from the software vendor and affiliates. Give a secondary email address in order to avoid receiving from the affiliate companies that share data such as email.

Activating a program is necessary. Registering a program is usually not mandatory, but has advantages.

14. LEARNING WINDOWS

Above is a Windows 10 screenshot. The look and feel is different from older versions of Windows and some users have issues adjusting to the user interface. Some people, especially seniors prefer the older menu-driven look of Windows 7.

Above is a screen shot from Classic Shell installed on a Windows system. As of this writing Classic Shell provides a nice user interface that is especially helpful for seniors. Classic Shell will automatically setup to work with Windows

Classic Shell can emulate many key elements, including the Start Menu, menus, wallpaper and taskbar. Upon installing, right click on the bottom icon where Classic Shell installed and select SETTINGS. Under setting, modifications to Classic Shell can be made.

WINDOWS HELP SCREENS

There are multiple approaches to help in Windows.

1. Enter the words "Help" or "Windows help" at the run command or into Cortana.
2. Enter the words "Windows Help" while on the Internet.
   Select any topic titled HELP and SUPPORT.
3. Click on any question mark

Windows provides online tutorials. These tutorials are very user friendly and can be found in the HELP Section.

MY PC

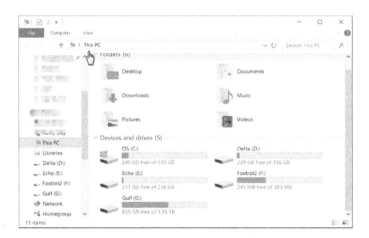

MY PC is an excellent source of information and should be an icon on the desktop. If Classic Shell was downloaded, MY PC can be accessed through the menu by clicking on the Start Button.

MY PC displays all drive and device sources of storage on the computer and available space on each. Notice all drives and external devices are lettered numerically and MY PC shows that the C drive has the operating system installed. Most computers will have the operating system installed on Drive C.

To setup an icon on the desktop, right click on the MY COMPUTER option in the menu and select CREATE SHORTCUT.

HOW TO BACKUP TO A FLASH DRIVE

When purchasing a flash drive or external hard drive for backup purposes, open up the MY PC screen first, then connect the external backup drive. In a few seconds, a new drive letter will appear. That new drive letter is the external backup where files are accessed and copied to.

CONTROL PANEL

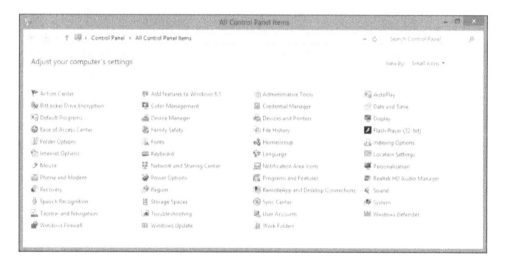

CONTROL PANEL is a widely used program that houses most of the Windows program functions. The more important programs include:

- DEVICE MANAGER provides information of each hardware device.
- PROGRAMS where programs are listed and uninstalled on the computer.
- RECOVERY (May be referred to as BACKUP AND RESTORE) is important. A user can setup a backup IMAGE or RESTORE POINT on the system.
- USER ACCOUNTS is where individual user accounts can be setup on the same computer. Restrictions of what each user can and cannot do.
- NETWORKING is where a user can configure network settings or setup a network.
- ADMINISTRATIVE is where more advanced system features are stored. Where Administrative Privileges can be assigned to different users, assuming more than one user has access to the computer.

CREATE A BACKUP IMAGE

An image backup copies everything on the hard drive—operating system, boot sector, programs, and data files—into one compressed but still very large file. If disaster renders the Windows installation useless, an image backup will allow a recovery to get the computer up and running again quickly. To create an image:

1. Plug in the external hard drive—which should have enough free space to hold everything on the internal drive. Make sure Windows can access the drive.
2. In Windows' Search field, type FILE HISTORY, and select Control Panel's FILE HISTORY PROGRAM program.
3. In the FILE HISTORY dialog box, select SYSTEM IMAGE BACKUP in the lower-left corner and follow the instructions.

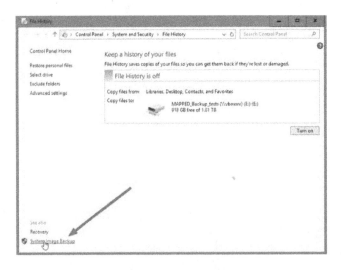

RESTORE AN IMAGE BACKUP

There are multiple ways to restore the Image Backup:

1. Start Windows: Select START/ SETTINGS / UPDATE AND SECURITY. Select RECOVERY / RESTART NOW.
2. If Windows won't boot:
   - Insert the Recovery media into the Drive or port and boot the PC.
   - If the PC skips the flash drive and attempts to boot Windows, reboot and enter the System Setup screen and look for boot order options.
   - Once in a recovery environment, select Troubleshoot, then System Image Recovery. Follow the instructions.

DEVICE MANAGER

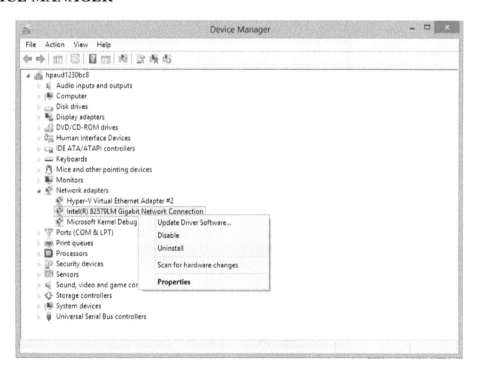

DEVICE MANAGER is commonly used to troubleshoot PC device-related problems. Device Manager will display if Windows correctly recognizes the computer devices. Devices in this screen shot look normal. Devices that are malfunctioning or have incorrect driver software will display a question mark or exclamation point on the driver. Right click on the driver to either ROLL BACK or UPDATE the driver software. Either option may correct a driver problem.

A device driver can be disabled, which means turned off. One example of disabling a driver is when a computer has an on-board video and a separate video card is added to the computer. The on-board video should be disabled to avoid any video driver conflict between the two video cards.

UPDATE drivers from the Device Manager screen. Minimally look to update the COMPUTER, DISPLAY, and NETWORK devices. Right click on each device / Select PROPERTIES and / Select UPDATE DRIVER. Windows will automatically look for an updated driver on the internet and update.

This is a safer way to update device drivers then downloading and installing Device Driver updater programs onto the computer. These types of free programs usually install other programs that could slow up or corrupt Windows on the system.

TASK MANAGER

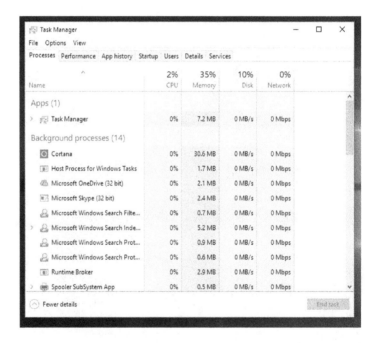

TASK MANAGER displays all processes running on the computer and how much system resource each process is taking. Task Manager can be useful if the computer begins to run slower or locks up. Individual program processes can be turned off until the process or program causing the problem is found. Unnecessary processes can be turned off here.

DEVICES & PRINTERS

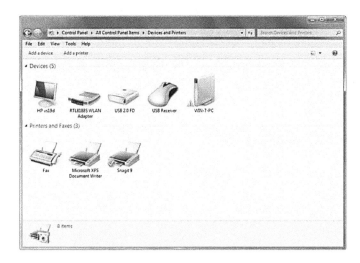

Devices and Printers is where most printing issues are addressed. RIGHT CLICK on the device having a problem and LEFT CLICK on PROPERTIES. A menu program will open with troubleshooting and maintenance options for that device. Printer maintenance can be accessed by right clicking on the type of printer ICON and left click on PROPERTIES.

DISK CLEANUP AND DISK DEFRAGMENTER

Disk Cleanup and Disk Defragmenter can be found under the Administrator / System tools.

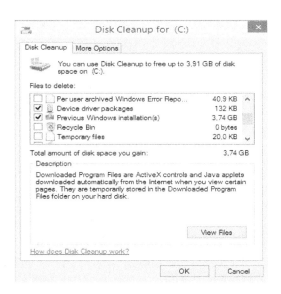

DISK CLEANUP is a computer maintenance utility designed to free up disk space on a computer's hard drive and remove junk from a computer. Run DISK CLEANUP once a month. Check every box and click on OK.

Run DISK CLEANUP at least twice consecutively. When running the second time, select to CLEAN SYSTEM FILES. Running Disk Cleanup multiple times does a better job of cleaning.

DISK DEFRAGMENTER

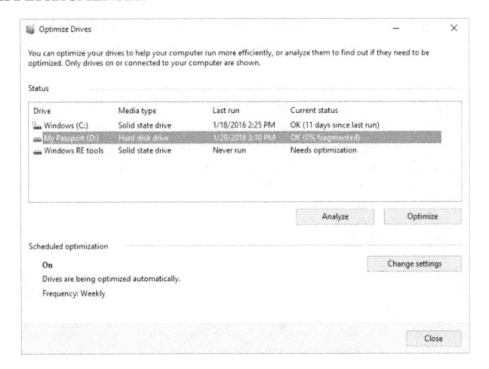

DISK DEFRAGMENTER rearranges and places files in logical order. Consider a disk defragment as spring cleaning on every system. Run the DISK DEFRAGMENTER right after the DISK CLEANUP once a month for optimal performance.

Fragmentation makes the hard disk perform extra work that can slow down a computer. Disk Defragmenter rearranges fragmented data so the hard drive works more efficiently. Disk Defragmenter might take from several minutes to a few hours to finish, depending on the size and degree of fragmentation of the hard disk. The computer can still be used during the defragmentation process; however, it may run slower. NOTE: Disk Defragmenter should NOT be run on SSD drives. Usually Windows will prompt a user not to run the Disk Defragmenter on an SSD drive.

WINDOWS UPDATES

Working on updates
11% complete
Don't turn off your computer

Most computer systems are automatically setup to accept Windows updates automatically. It is a good idea to automatically let Windows update the computer, because most of the updates are security updates for the Edge or Explorer browser.

Usually a backup restore point is setup prior to the update so the computer can be recovered in the event of a problem with the updates. It is a good idea to manually check for Windows updates at least once a month. To manually check enter PC SETTINGS / Select WINDOWS UPDATES / and pick CHECK FOR UPDATES.

EDGE & EXPLORER INTERNET BROWSERS

INTERNET EXPLORER   MICROSOFT EDGE

Windows 10 now includes Microsoft Edge as the default system browser. Windows 8 and earlier versions includes Internet Explorer. Microsoft Edge is accessed by clicking on the lower Taskbar; however, can be accessed through a menu under Apps.

Older versions of Windows including Windows 8 and older cannot run Microsoft Edge. They can run Microsoft Explorer Version 11. Consider using Google Chrome on older versions of Windows for security reasons.

PROGRAMS

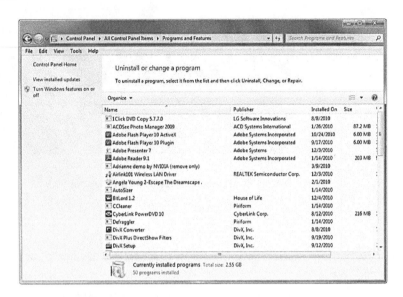

PROGRAMS are where programs on the computer can be uninstalled. PROGRAMS can be accessed under CONTROL PANEL.

WINDOWS APPS

Windows Apps are basically other programs within Windows. Microsoft is attempting to provide the same user interfaces across computers, touchscreens and phones. Microsoft placed some programs such as PAINT and DEFENDER SECURITY CENTER. The CAMERA is probably the most used App. Become familiar with the Apps within Windows.

LOCATING ADDITIONAL FREE (and Pay) WINDOWS APPS

The Microsoft website has many apps for Windows for purchase and free. It is best to setup a Microsoft Account (which is free) to access and download Apps from the Microsoft site.

TO DOWNLOAD AND INSTALL APPS FROM THE MICROSOFT SITE

1. Launch the Store from the Start menu.
2. Click the user icon next to the search box.
3. Click "Sign-in" from the menu that appears.
4. Choose "Microsoft account" and log in like normal. One has to setup a Microsoft Account to access Apps, but the account is free.
5. When the "Make it yours" box appears, do not enter a password. Instead, click "Sign in to just this app instead."

ACCESSORIES

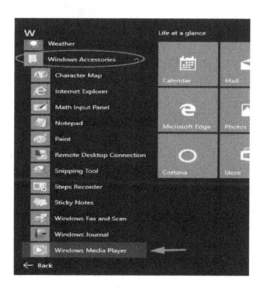

The ACCESSORIES Folder in Windows has useful programs; however, these programs are not critical on using or repairing a system in the event of a problem. Review these programs at your convenience.

USER ACCOUNTS

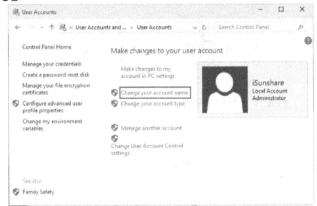

USER ACCOUNTS can be located under CONTROL PANEL. USER ACCOUNTS permit individual accounts to be setup on the computer. The main user of the computer should be setup as the ADMINISTRATOR on the computer. The administrator can override any user or user password on the system. Make sure the main account is setup with ADMINSTRATOR Privileges. Check under SETTINGS.

Unless information is top secret, avoid passwords on user accounts. Passwords usually cause more problems than they are worth. If the computer becomes unusable and the hard drive must be removed to save data, if accounts were password protected, the data may be Permissioned.

Permissioned means that while the hard drive works, the data is still not be accessible because with the hard drive pulled, the password placed on the user account is still active and special programs have to be run to remove the account password.

RIGHT CLICK OPTIONS

The Right Click Menu or the Context Menu is the menu, which appears when right-clicking on the desktop or a file or folder in Windows. This menu gives added functionality. Right clicking is mostly used to create a new file folder for storing data or changing the graphic look or computer display resolution.

WINDOWS TROUBLESHOOTER

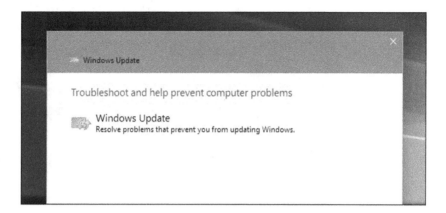

Windows can troubleshoot and correct many problems. Assuming Windows is working, the Troubleshooter can be accessed under PC SETTINGS.

Microsoft has Troubleshooting programs on their website. Microsoft has an entire Troubleshooting area at their website titled THE MICROSOFT FIXIT SOLUTION CENTER.

Microsoft has problems listed online by categories. Troubleshooter may ask questions or reset common settings as it works to correct the problem.

If the troubleshooter repairs the problem, close it. If Troubleshooter couldn't correct the problem, it may provide several options that can be tried online. The complete list of changes made can be viewed.

SAFE MODE

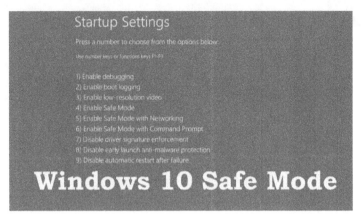

SAFE MODE is accessed by restarting the computer once turned on and hold down the [Shift] key on the keyboard when clicking Restart. Safe mode on older computers is accessed by pressing F8 on start-up. The Safe mode screen on an older computer will be black, not blue.

Windows Safe Mode is a very basic stripped down version of Windows. Safe Mode does not load programs or hardware device drivers when starting. Safe Mode is a very good base line test to determine the level of problem.

Windows operating in Safe Mode will have reduced functionality, but the task of isolating problems is easier because many non-core components are disabled. An installation that will only boot into its safe mode typically has a problem, such as disk corruption or the installation of poorly configured software that prevents the operating system from successfully booting into its normal operating mode.

Safe Mode has an option to boot to the Recovery Console for Windows re-installation or to various "safe mode" options that run the dysfunctional operating system, but with features such as video drivers, audio and networking disabled. Re-install Windows if the computer doesn't work in Safe Mode, this rule holds true for all versions of Windows.

If the computer does not start in Windows Safe Mode, Windows should be re-installed.

Do not attempt to repair the system other than to re-install Windows. Attempting any other repair is similar to having a hospital splint a broken ankle instead of casting it.

SYSTEM BIOS or SETUP SCREEN

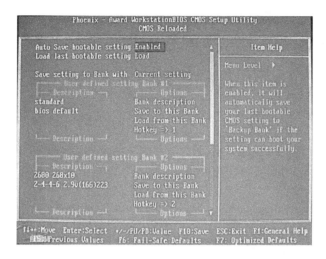

The Setup utility program is a set of firmware programs stored in a battery in the computer. Setup stores system settings in a battery located on the system motherboard. Setup is NOT part of Windows or the operating system.

ACCESS THE SETUP UTILITY

Setup is accessed differently depending on the computer. Usually the computer will give a prompt on startup. The most common keystrokes used would be F1, F2, F10, the DELETE, or ESCAPE keys immediately after starting the computer. If the system starts Windows, the keys to enter Safe Mode were not pressed early enough. The main reasons to access the Setup programs are:

1. **CHANGE THE DEVICE BOOT ORDER**

    The Bios can change the Device Boot order, for example have the computer boot or start from a flash drive or DVD drive instead of the hard drive. This is at times necessary if Windows needs to be re-installed from a DVD or flash drive.

2. RESET OR CHANGE THE DATE AND TIME

The date and time on the computer must be correct to download Windows updates. If a BIOS battery is failing or beginning to fail, the system may lose date and time and must be reset.

3. RUN HARDWARE DIAGNOSTICS

Certain Setup programs have their own hardware diagnostic programs that can test the memory and hard drive. Hardware diagnostics can be run within Setup only if the Setup program can be accessed. The tests may not be reliable if the problem is motherboard related.

4. CREATE A SYSTEM PASSWORD

A system password can be setup to prevent user access to the system. NOTE: A system password is more secure than a Windows password; however, can be extremely difficult to remove if a person forgets the password or was changed without their knowledge. It is NOT recommended using a SYSTEM password.

5. LOAD SYSTEM DEFAULTS

A System or Bios is stored in a CMOS battery that is attached to a motherboard. These batteries eventually wear out, similar to a car battery. A failing CMOS battery can cause all kinds of unusual problems with a computer. Weird things happen because a failing CMOS battery cannot keep the system settings in place to properly run the computer.

6. CHANGE THE TYPE OF WINDOWS RE-INSTALLATION

Certain computers may need to change from UEFI to Legacy booting in order to re-install Windows. Do some homework prior to changing these settings.

Learn basic Windows operations to make your computing life easier.

15. COMMON PROBLEMS AND SOLUTIONS

Listed are the most common problems we encounter and the steps we take to solve each problem. If unsure how to apply these corrections, additional information can be accessed online by researching the problem using the Internet.

1. COMPUTER RUNS SLOW

a) Was the computer always slow or did it slow up recently? If the computer was slow from the beginning, the hard drive may be failing or the system was underpowered or junked up.

b) Check the system specifications to make sure there is enough memory and free hard drive space. This can be an issue with these new low cost netbooks with only 32 or 64 gig SSD hard drives.

c) Too many programs are loading in Startup. Uninstall or get into the STARTUP and turn off unnecessary programs running in STARTUP. A free program like Glary Utilities allows a user to easily get into the System Startup and turn off programs.

d) If the hard drive is near capacity, the system will slow down. The hard drive should be at least 33% empty. Scan the hard drive to check for bad sectors using Active or Ultimate Boot Disk.

e) Scan the computer for viruses or spyware.

f) Run DISK CLEANUP and DISK DEFRAGMENTER. Do NOT run the disk defragmenter if the hard drive is SSD.

g) Boot into the computer SETUP utility and run the hard drive diagnostic test program.
h) Download and run the Microsoft FIXIT program.
i) Re-install Windows and be sure to format the hard drive during the process.

2. CANNOT ACCESS THE INTERNET

IF THE PROBLEM IS <u>BOTH WIRED AND WIRELESS</u>

a) Reset the modem / router by turning off power for 20 seconds. Pull the modem / router power plug and replace. Restart the modem first, then the computer.
b) Reset the web browser settings. Open browser / Click on top right / SETTINGS /ADVANCED / RESET or CLEAR BROWSER.
c) Check for viruses, spyware and malware. Clear the browser settings.
d) Turn on the computer and test the Internet in SAFE MODE WITH NETWORKING. Attempt to access Internet again.
e) A software firewall program may be preventing Internet access. Turn off or uninstall any and all security suites. Check the taskbar to make sure the programs are turned off.
f) Use a different computer to isolate the problem. Be sure that the problem is not with the Internet provider. If multiple computers cannot access the Internet, call the Internet Provider.

IF THE PROBLEM IS <u>WIRELESS ONLY</u>

a) Is the wireless device ON? Check wireless switches or buttons.
b) Does the notebook see any wireless connections? If other wireless networks are being seen and available, there may be a problem with your wireless network.
c) Right click on the wireless icon on the bottom right of the Taskbar and run REPAIR.
d) If the Repair doesn't work, power off, re-power the computer and try again.
e) Re-power the modem and wireless router (if being used) and computer. Restart the modem first and the computer last.
f) Take a notebook elsewhere and attempt to access a different wireless network or use a different wireless computer on the network to isolate the problem to either the computer or the network.
g) Check Device Manager for bad or missing wireless network drivers.
h) Restart the computer in SAFE MODE and attempt to get on the Internet using Safe Mode with Networking.
i) Check for viruses, spyware and malware.
j) Are there any obstructions or signal conflicts that may inhibit the wireless connection?

INTERNET BROWSER PROBLEMS

Spyware and other destructive programs get embedded into the web browser and is the reason a user cannot access the internet. Follow the browser tips below.

KEEP MULTIPLE BROWSERS ON A COMPUTER

Keep at least two browsers on the computer. Any Windows system will by default include either Edge or Internet Explorer if the system is older. Download and keep Google Chrome, Firefox or all three as backup browsers in case of a problem.

If for some reason the computer won't get onto the Internet, close the browser being used and open an alternate browser to access the Internet. If the alternative browser gets on the Internet, the problem is with the first browser. If both browsers don't work, the problem could be with the Internet service or a virus on the computer.

LEARN TO RESET THE BROWSER

Most browsers can be reset the same way. Using either Microsoft Edge or Google Chrome, click on the top right of the screen to get to SETTINGS. Search for CLEAR SETTINGS OR CLEAR BROWSER DATA.

The picture on the next page shows where to click in the Microsoft Edge browser to clear the browser settings. This commonly corrects minor internet access issues. Clearing the browser will clear all the downloaded junk files out that cause most of these problems.

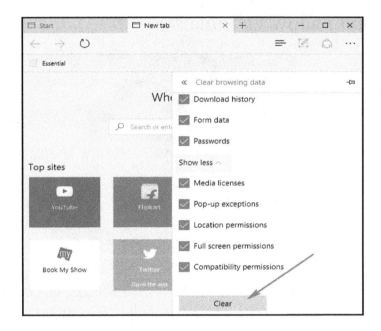

To clear a browser:

- Click on the three dots at the top right of the open browser
- Search for CLEAR BROWSER.
- Select the option to CLEAR at least two to three times.

3. COMPUTER POWERS UP BUT DOESN'T START WINDOWS

a) Check that a bootable external device isn't causing the problem. Remove all DVD or flash drives from the system that may be causing a start-up problem.
b) Remove all power to the computer, turn back on and restart again.
c) Restart the computer in SAFE MODE. If Windows starts in SAFE MODE, the problem is probably software related – virus, spyware or device driver issue that may be fixable without re-installing. If computer does not restart in SAFE MODE, re-install Windows.
d) Restart the computer with a bootable Windows Repair media. Run REPAIR YOUR COMPUTER.
e) Turn off power, unplug and reconnect both the mouse and keyboard. Use a replacement mouse and keyboard. If the problem happened immediately after a WINDOWS UPDATE or DEVICE DRIVER UPDATE, attempt to ROLL BACK the driver in Device Manager.

4. NO PICTURE ON THE SCREEN

a) Power off both computer and monitor and restart the monitor first and then the computer.
b) Check that the computer is not in HIBERNATION or POWER SAVE mode and asleep. Press a key on the keyboard and wait up to one minute for a response.
c) Check power to the computer and LCD monitor.
d) Check the cable connection from the LCD monitor to the computer.
e) Check that cable is connected to the correct video output if the system has multiple video ports.
f) Use a different monitor on the computer or connect the notebook to an external monitor to test for video.

5. WINDOWS ERROR MESSAGE

a) Does the message say anything about a bad hard drive or bad memory? If so test or replace either the memory or hard drive. Reseat the memory or replace the memory in a different memory slot.
b) Turn off the computer, re-connect the mouse and keyboard and re-start the computer.
c) Power the computer off, disconnect all peripheral devices connected and restart the computer without any device connections. If the computer restarts, add a single device on each restart to determine which device is causing the problem.
d) Start up and run in SAFE MODE. If the computer doesn't startup in Safe Mode, re-install Windows.
e) Check for and remove viruses, spyware and malware.
f) If the last thing done prior to the problem was a Windows or driver update, undo the last update.
g) Attempt to roll back the video driver or last device driver updated.
h) Download and run the Microsoft FIXIT program.

6. NO SOUND

a) Check that the speaker connector cable is plugged into correct spot on the soundcard (green color, SPK or OUT)
b) Check that speakers have power, are turned on and volume control knob is turned up at least half way.
c) Click on the Speaker Icon on the Taskbar. Check that the sound isn't MUTED or volume set to a very low setting.
d) Attempt to use the speakers on a different computer.

e) Check Device Manager and be sure there aren't any sound device driver conflicts or problems. If there are, attempt to either ROLL BACK, UPDATE or RE-INSTALL the sound driver.

f) If the Speaker Icon is missing on the Taskbar, the soundcard may be physically bad and needs to be replaced or Windows may be corrupted and needs to be re-installed.

g) A notebook may have a physical switch or control for sound. Check that the switch is on and the control volume is turned up at least half way.

7. INTERNAL OR EXTERNAL DEVICE DOESN'T WORK

a) Check DEVICE MANAGER for any conflicts.

b) Re-install the device by deleting the device and let Windows find the device during installation.

c) Install the device using the manufacturer's driver CD or download from the manufacturer website.

d) If upgraded to a newer version of Windows, check that the device has the correct drivers. Computer components have different device drivers for different versions of Windows

e) Start the computer in SAFE MODE and see what happens.

f) Contact the manufacturer for an updated driver.

g) Move the device to a different slot inside the computer or with different cables.

h) Replace the device in a different slot or USB port.

i) Run HARDWARE TROUBLESHOOTER.

j) Download and run the Microsoft FIXIT program.

k) Try a replacement device.

8. NOTEBOOK WON'T POWER UP

a) Physically remove the notebook battery from the notebook and restart.

b) Check if the AC charger displays a solid green light. If not attempt using a replacement power supply.

c) Connect an LCD monitor to the notebook video port connection and restart the computer. On start-up, press the notebook Function Key along with the Dual Monitor key (Usually F 4 or F5 key) simultaneously. If an image appears on the external monitor, the notebook has an LCD screen problem or inverter problem.

d) If the jack connection is loose or can be wiggled, the jack has to be re-soldered or replaced.

9. PRINTER DOESN'T PRINT

   a) Restart the printer and computer.
   b) Check that the printer cartridges have ink left in the cartridges
   c) Uninstall and re-install the printer driver software.
   d) Print out directly from the printer without using the computer.
   e) Print a Windows Test Page to determine if the problem is with Windows or the application program on the computer.
   f) Install the printer on a different computer to determine if the problem is with the printer or the computer.

10. BLINKING CURSOR ONLY WHEN STARTING UP THE COMPUTER

   a) Check that there isn't a non-bootable media (DVD or USB flash drive) attached to the computer. If so, remove it and restart the computer.
   b) Boot up using a bootable utility program and scan the hard drive. Find out if the bootable program sees the system.
   c) Attempt to enter the SETUP OR BIOS program on startup and select LOAD SETUP DEFAULT VALUES, save the changes and restart the computer. Take the computer to a repair shop if the system will not even get into the SETUP program on startup.
   d) Attempt a complete Windows re-installation.

11. ACCIDENTLY DELETED A FILE THAT WAS IMPORTANT

   A file in the RECYCLE BIN is retrievable so long as the Recycle Bin wasn't emptied. Open the RECYCLE BIN, select the file to restore back on the computer and select RESTORE.

12. WINDOWS NOT STARTING UP

   a) Wait at least 5 minutes. Windows may be completing updates on a restart.
   b) Press the <ENTER> key a couple of times to make sure that the computer just isn't in the middle of a process.
   c) Unplug all USB connection devices, press and hold down the POWER BUTTON, wait until computer is off and
   d) Press the power button again to restart.
   e) Re-install Windows.

Most Answers can be found online.

16. COMMON ERROR MESSAGES

Listed below are some common error messages and their meanings.

ACCESS DENIED

This error occurs if the user doesn't have sufficient security privileges to access the file or program. Set the main account as the Administrator. The person with Administrator privileges should be able to gain access to most Windows files or programs. Other users can be setup with Administrative privileges under CONTROL PANEL / USERS.

ACTIVATION PERIOD HAS ENDED or PLEASE ACTIVATE

Windows or the program being used must be activated to continue program use. Activation is the process used to verify that a legal copy of the program is being used.

If the computer is licensed, the owner has a right to use that licensed version of Windows on that computer. Application programs need to be activated. Trial versions usually shut down after thirty days forcing the user to purchase the program or not use the program.

BAD COMMAND OR FILENAME

The computer doesn't understand the command. Most likely the user keyed in the wrong filename or command. Check the spelling, spacing and make sure separation hyphens (/) are being correctly placed.

BLUE SCREEN OF DEATH ERROR

A blue screen error message means Windows has a problem and won't work properly. Read the message to get an indication of the problem and Google the message. Start Windows in SAFE MODE to see if the same error occurs.

DEVICE NOT READY

Windows is attempting to access an external USB device, CD or DVD or floppy drive that cannot be read either because the device isn't ready, setup properly or there isn't readable media in the drive. The user may be attempting to access the drive too quickly and the drive or program is slow to respond. First be patient and then open the drive, soft cloth clean a CD or DVD, re-insert and try again.

DLL ERROR or MISSING DLL FILE

Most DLL errors are usually minor software errors in the system Registry that usually results from a program either not properly installed or uninstalled from a computer. Run a program like Glary Utilities or Cccleaner to remove DLL errors.

DRIVE NOT AVAILABLE or MISSING STORAGE DEVICE ON STARTUP

Windows doesn't see the storage device; this message may occur during startup and Windows is attempting to load and access the hard drive. Restart the computer and check that there isn't any external boot up devices attached – flash drives, external hard drives or CD in the CD drive.

ERROR READING DRIVE C

An indication there is a physical problem with the computer's hard drive. Attempt to get into the System Setup and run a hard drive diagnostic test.

FILE NOT FOUND

Either Windows cannot find the file, the file is damaged, deleted or could have been moved to a different location on the computer. Check the file spelling. The file should not be caps sensitive.

INVALID DATE / TIME

A PC with this error message usually has a failing CMOS battery on the motherboard that should be replaced. A computer with this problem can be used, just key in the correct date and time each time it's turned on and save the changes. It's like jumping a failing car battery. A desktop CMOS battery is easy to replace; however, a notebook CMOS battery (not charging battery) can be difficult to replace.

Having an incorrect date or time on the computer can prevent Windows updates from installing. Manually change the date and time in Windows by clicking on the calendar at the bottom right of the screen.

LOW DISK SPACE

This error occurs when the hard drive is full OR a partition on the hard drive is full. This will happen frequently with the netbooks with only 32 or 64 gig SSD drives for storage. Run DISK CLEANUP to free up drive space. If the C drive is full, remove data to free up space or reformat the hard drive and re-install Windows.

MEMORY ERROR referenced at _____

This error may indicate that a bad memory chip. First reseat the memory or place the memory in a different memory slot.

NO OPERATING SYSTEM

The operating system cannot be found on startup. This message indicates one of the following:

- The hard drive may be failing.
- Windows was deleted from the system.
- The computer is attempting to start-up from an external device that doesn't have Windows installed, such as a flash drive.
- Someone may have tried to re-install or upgrade Windows and did not complete the process.

NON-SYSTEM DISK ERROR

This error occurs when attempting to boot the computer from a non-bootable CD, DVD or USB external flash or hard drive on start-up. Remove all CDs from the system, disconnect all external USB flash and hard drives and attempt again.

OUT OF MEMORY

This error occurs when the system has run out of memory or tries to load a file too large to store in RAM which is temporary memory. One possible correction is to close additional programs loading on startup or install additional memory.

FATAL EXCEPTION ERROR

A fatal exception error or fatal error is an error that causes a program to abort and may therefore return the user to the operating system. When this happens, data that the program was processing may be lost. Usually this message is caused by a program error, memory or device driver conflict problem.

ANY ERROR MESSAGE NOT LISTED HERE

GOOGLE any message not listed or understood. Windows 7 will call attention to a problem through its problem reporter. A message will display on the bottom right of the task bar explaining the problem.

Listed above are the most common error messages. Google any unknown message not found here.

17. COMPUTER MYTHS

Computer myths that we will dispel:

1. **A system with an updated anti-virus program installed won't get viruses.**

    FALSE. No one anti-virus program stops all destructive files and programs out there. Certain programs are better preventing viruses, other programs combat spyware and malware, but any type of destructive program can cause problems with a computer. Almost 20,000 new viruses are released weekly and it takes a little time for the virus protection to catch up.

    Remember the old vampire movies? Once the vampire was asked into the home, the asker had a problem. When a user clicks on the wrong link, the problem will bypass all the system protection and get onto the computer. Be careful when selecting a link.

    It doesn't matter how many anti-virus or protection programs are running on the computer if the wrong link or item is selected. That problem program will bypass all the computer protection and screw up the computer.

2. **A system will be better protected if multiple anti-virus programs are installed.**

   FALSE. The system is no better protected PLUS a computer multiple anti-virus programs on a system will slow down the system, because the competing programs fight for control of the system, slowing it down while they battle it out for system supremacy.

3. **Anti-virus software will automatically update, so I don't have to worry about it.**

   FALSE. We have removed viruses from many computers with current versions of an anti-virus program that did not have the latest updates. To be safe manually update and run the anti-virus program at least once a month. It's not a bad idea to manually update Windows and protection programs at least once a month.

4. **All programs will be installed back on the computer if Windows is re-installed.**

   MAYBE. If the re-installation originated from a manufacturer image, the re-installation should include all programs originally installed on the computer when originally purchased. Any program installed after the Image or restore point was created will need to be installed again from original installation media.

5. **Backed up files and programs to a different hard drive will work exactly the same.**

   PROBABLY NOT. If a complete backup of the ENTIRE original hard drive is copied to an external hard drive the data should be getable; however, any copied programs may not work right. Usually programs must be re-installed from scratch and copied programs will not work correctly.

6. **It's all right to move a notebook while it's on.**

   FALSE. Notebooks are now being made using SSD flash drive technology because the older hard drives have spindles that can be moved out of alignment when the notebook is powered on and being moved.

   Our service centers have performed more hard drive replacements in notebooks than any other type of repair. Power the notebook off prior to moving it or even lowering the screen. Treat any notebook similar to a record player playing a record. Turn the notebook off prior to moving it.

7. **It's OK to use a notebook on the bed or on a lap.**

FALSE. A bed, couch or lap blocks notebook air-flow vents which produces heat internally. Purchase a notebook cooling pad ($20-30) to place under the notebook which will stabilize the notebook and help keep it cool.

8. **Data converts from a PC to a MAC with little problem.**

NOT ALWAYS TRUE. Pictures and music are no problem; however, data may be an issue. Look into data conversion before switching from a PC to Apple or Apple to PC. Programs such as Microsoft Office may need to be repurchased.

9. **I no longer use UTorrent, Torrentz or Limewire (free illegal file sharing sites) anymore, so my computer should be free of viruses.**

FALSE. Even when discontinuing using a file sharing sites, the computer is still more susceptible to viruses and it's possible to get re-infected. Malware is similar to roaches. The bug exterminator can fumigate a home; however, if one roach survives, he will send out a signal to his roach buddies that the coast is clear to return. We recommend to any user that has used those sites to remove them and run full virus, malware and spyware scans.

10. **Using 3rd party printer inks void a printer warranty.**

FALSE. The printer manufacturers attempt to scare users into using their ink only, because the ink is their cash cow. Save money and use either ink refills or re-manufactured ink refills.

11. **The cheapest inkjet printer probably has the least expensive replacement Inks.**

FALSE. Usually the cheapest inkjet printers generally require the most expensive inks. Before purchasing any printer, price out the replacement ink or toner first.

12. **Its O.K. to unplug a flash drive from the computer while on.**

Don't plug or unplug a flash drive without first safely allowing the flash drive to be removed. Select the flash drive icon on the bottom right of the taskbar and click on SAFELY REMOVE FLASH DRIVE.

13. A replacement monitor must be from the same manufacturer.

FALSE. Monitors, mice, keyboards can be used on most Windows based PCs so long as the connections are correct.

14. Using Torrent downloading files illegally but have undated anti-virus software on the computer makes the computer safe.

FALSE. File sharing programs grab pieces of the requested file for download within the Torrent user group (called seeders). It's most likely a seeder has an infected file that may download past an anti-virus program.

15. Higher priced video cables make the HDTV look better.

Not necessarily. PC World ran tests and found no difference between bargain basement cables and expensive ones. Purchase the less expensive cables first and only purchase expensive cabling if dissatisfied with the results.

16. All drives must be defragmented regularly.

FALSE. Standard hard drives should be defragmented at least once every two months. Solid state drives do not have a drive platter or read / write heads that need to constantly search the hard drive, so they do not need to be defragmented. It's not a good idea to defragment solid state drives (SSD).

Don't believe everything you read or are told about computers.

18. PC TUNE-UP & GENERAL HOUSEKEEPING

MODERN SYMPATHY CARDS

Computers are like cars in that they require on-going maintenance to work properly. Most people don't drive their car 50,000 without an oil change? In this chapter we discuss upgrades and tweaks that may improve computer performance.

ADD MEMORY

Adding additional memory in many cases will improve performance. Memory isn't expensive and is easy to install.

TURN OFF PROGRAMS IN STARTUP

A computer can lag if too many programs are loading into Startup. Programs can be disabled under TASK MANAGER or using a third party program like Glary Utilities. Do not turn off any Microsoft programs unless you are sure what that particular program does.

DON'T DUPLICATE

Only run one anti-virus and one spyware removal program. Multiple programs don't provide additional protection and in fact slow down a system because they will fight for system control.

CHECK FOR SPYWARE and MALWARE

Spyware and Malware slow up a computer. Scan the system with updated spyware and malware removal software. It's a good idea to always get updates on the protection software, prior to running scans, so the system is being checked with the latest version of the protection.

UNINSTALL UNNECESSARY PROGRAMS

Uninstall any unnecessary programs. New computers may be loaded with junk programs, most of which will never be used. Junk or invasive programs take up room on the hard drive and may cause a lag in computer response time if they are loading on startup. Uninstall unnecessary programs in CONTROL PANEL / PROGRAMS / and select REMOVE.

CHECK SYSTEM RESOURCES

To get started with Resource Monitor, press Windows +R, type Resmon.exe in the Open text box, and press Enter. In the Resource Monitor user interface, select the STARTUP tab.

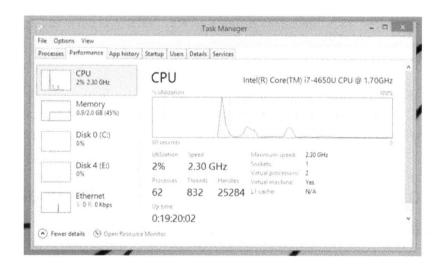

All programs starting up will be shown along with resource taken. Turn off any unnecessary program.

RUN DISK CLEANUP and DISK DEFRAGMENTER

Run Windows DISK CLEANUP and DISK DEFRAGMENTER at least once a month. Do NOT run disk defragmenter on a Solid State drive.

GET WINDOWS AND DEVICE DRIVER UPDATES

Check for Windows updates. To get the latest updates for hardware devices, right click on each individual device and select UPDATE DRIVER. Windows will automatically search for the latest driver for the device.

Another option is to visit each driver manufacturer website; however, letting Windows automatically search for device drivers is easier.

RUN REGISTRY AND OPTIMIZER PROGRAMS

Download and run free registry and optimizer programs, like Cccleaner and Glary Utilities. They work very well with cleaning the registry and removing junk programs.

EMPTY THE RECYCLE BIN

Manually empty the Recycle Bin at least every six months. When a file is deleted, it moves to the Recycle Bin but isn't deleted, at least not right away. Check the Recycle Bin prior to emptying it. Check that nothing important is being deleted. Once the Recycle Bin is emptied, everything that was in there is permanently removed.

BACKUP CRITICAL FILES

HOW OFTEN: Every time changes are made to the documents. A backup may take up to 60 seconds. Backing up the entire USER folder will save documents, music and photos.

Follow these rules for General Housekeeping to make your computing life easier.

19. COMPUTER PARENTING

The last thing anyone should ever do is tell a parent how to raise their child and that includes computers. I decided to take a less invasive approach in this chapter and list my daughter's computer milestones and life experiences. This section may be of interest of those with children or even grandchildren.

My daughter Annie started on computers at four. Her first computer was one of those plastic toy store computers. She quickly lost interest in that and of course had to use mine. At preschool, she progressed with educational programs. Her favorite was Putt Putt the car. Putt Putt must have saved all the animals in that zoo over 100 times.

Start training youngsters on education programs ASAP. Educational games are a great tool for building foundation math and language skills that today's elementary school curriculum requires. To find online children's sites, simply perform an Internet search for "Children's educational games"

Children don't have to be on the Internet to use an interactive educational program. Children's educational games are still available on DVD. These older programs usually operate on older systems without any difficulty.

TEENAGERS AND SOCIAL NETWORKING

Teenagers will be social networking on a computer. Those still living in the 19th century, social networking is meeting online, usually on Facebook, Twitter, Pinterest, or Instagram.

CHECK THE BROWSER HISTORY

If concerned about tracking your children's movements on the Internet, view where they've been by looking at their browser history.

TO VIEW BROWSER HISTORY

To view the browser history, just click on the down arrow to the right of the search / input box. If the browser history has been cleared, you have a problem because:

- They are smart enough to do it and
- They are clearing their browser history because they know someone won't approve of the websites they are visiting.

PARENTAL CONTROLS

Parental controls are features included in digital television services, phones, and computer software. Parental controls fall into roughly four categories, content filters, which limit access to age appropriate content and usage that limit the usage of these devices such as placing time-limits or forbidding certain types of usage, computer usage management tools, which allow parents to enforce learning time into child computing time, and monitoring, which can track location and activity when using the devices.

Get teenagers a separate computer so they don't screw up yours. Good luck attempting to monitor them online.

20. VIRUSES, SPYWARE AND MALWARE

A virus is a computer program that can copy itself and infect a computer. A virus can spread from one computer to another because a user sent it over a network, the Internet, or passed it on through a flash drive or removable medium. Viruses are purposely written to cause problems with computers. Viruses attach and infect a computer through email attachments and through clicking on web links. Viruses cause all types of problems with a system.

HOW VIRUSES GET ON A COMPUTER

Most software problems access a computer through the Internet. Bad stuff can gain access to a computer through an email attachment or a web link that was clicked on. Once that link or attachment is selected, in many cases the anti-virus protection doesn't catch the problem file and the computer will be infected. Beware on clicking advertisements on social networking sites.

HOW TO DECIDE THE COMPUTER IS INFECTED

The computer isn't working correctly. Virus related symptoms include any of the following:

- Popups that won't disappear.
- A program popup stating that a virus is on the computer and it will cost $49.99 - $250.00 to get the virus removed from the system.
- The web browser won't open.
- Blue screens.
- Unable to access the Internet.
- System is slow or crashes.

DOES ONE PROGRAM PROTECT AGAINST EVERYTHING?

NO. Different types of removal tools remove different types of problems. It's best to have different types of removal tool programs, but not multiple programs of the same type. For example, install and use separate anti-virus and spyware removal programs, but not two different anti-virus programs on the same computer.

Two similar programs probably overlap on protection; however, not necessarily provide better protection and slow down the computer. Both anti-virus programs fight for control of the computer and slow down the computer.

When our store would clean a computer, we would run between 6-8 different removal tools to clean computers. No single program will protect a computer from every destructive file.

20,000 – 40,000 PER WEEK

Each week anywhere between 20 and 40,000 new destructive computer files are released. It can take weeks or months for the protection programs to develop an antidote (removal tool). It's a good idea to always update whatever protection program being used prior to running it on a computer.

VIRUS PHONE SCAMS

A person will call on the phone stating they are from Microsoft and that your computer is infected and you need to pay them to fix it. The phone scams are usually targeted at seniors. Microsoft typically will not solicit. Unless you initiated the contact with the company, you are probably being setup to be scammed.

SPYWARE

SPYWARE is a type of malware that once installed on computers, collects small pieces of information about users without their knowledge. Spyware programs can collect various types of user personal information such as Internet surfing habits and sites visited, but can interfere with user control of the computer in other ways, such as installing additional software and redirecting the Internet web browser. Spyware can change computer settings, resulting in slow connection speeds, different home pages, or loss of web access.

WHY SPYWARE IS PLACED ON COMPUTERS

Most advertising links on websites are advertisers that pay the website for any referral web traffic sent to them. Websites get reimbursed for marketing demographics they capture and provide to advertisers. Advertisers are interested how long a user stayed at a site, pages visited and the types of sites visited for marketing strategies. Spyware tracks a computer Internet movement and relays the information back to the site for processing.

MALWARE

MALWARE, short for malicious software was designed to secretly access a computer system without the owner's knowledge. The writer of a malware program intended the program to cause problems with a computer, once it gains access. Malware includes viruses, worms, Trojan horses, spyware, scare ware, hijackers, rootkits and other malicious and unwanted software or program. MALWARE is destructive spyware.

Malware typically causes problem with the Windows browser or Internet access. Malware has a tendency to affect the Windows operating system directly, while Spyware tends to junk up the web browser; however, both malware and spyware cause programs.

RANDSOMEWARE

Ransomware is a type of malware that restricts access to a computer and demands that the user pay a ransom to the hackers to remove the restriction. Examples include:

- Locker ransomware: typically spread through social media sites.
- Crypto ransomware: Instead of restricting user action by denying access to the computer.

If a computer gets ransomware and files are backed up, reload Windows and wipe everything off the drive. Otherwise removing Ransomware can be a hard job.

WHAT ARE THE BEST PROGRAMS TO USE?

We prefer free programs over the pay packages. The biggest advantage of pay protection programs is that they update their protection definitions on a more frequent basis than free programs, but as a consumer, I can live with daily definition protection updates instead of hourly updates if the program is free.

OUR FREE FAVORITES

Some programs may ask about upgrading to their professional versions for a cost. We do not believe upgrading to a pay version is necessary in most cases; however, weigh the additional benefits and make your own decision.

Microsoft Defender

Windows Defender is malware protection that is included with and built into Windows. Defender helps identify and remove viruses, spyware and destructive programs. Windows Defender runs in the background and notifies a user when there is a problem and the need to take specific action.

A manual scan can be run any time if the computer isn't working properly. Microsoft Security Essentials is a nice basic program that does a good job for older versions of Windows.

Rkill

RKill is a program that was developed at BleepingComputer.com. Rkill attempts to terminate known malware processes so that your normal security software can then run and clean a computer of infections. Run RKILL first and then begin to run your spyware and malware removal programs.

RKill only terminates a program's running process and does not delete any files. After completing Rkill, begin running other protection software and do not restart the computer. Any malware processes that are configured to start automatically will just be started again.

Superantispyware

Superantispyware is at the top of the list because of its effectiveness and longevity. Superantispyware has been removing spyware for a long time and still provides the best overall bang for the buck in terms of the number of problems it finds and removes. Superantispyware is a very good program for cleaning web browsers.

Malwarebytes

Malwarebytes focuses mostly on Malware type problems, not a program to run as primary or the only protection. Malwarebytes focuses more on programs that affect the operating system.

Adwcleaner

Adwcleaner is a useful program to remove adware, bloatware, unwanted toolbars, and other potentially unwanted programs (PUPs) from a Windows PC.

Junkware Removal Tool

JRT is another removal security utility that searches for and removes common adware, toolbars, and potentially unwanted programs (PUPs) from a computer.

Combofix

A wonderful program provided by bleepingcomputer.com. Combofix can only be used on Windows 7 and older versions of Windows.

Other Good Removal Tools

Other good free utilities include Avast, Alvira Anti-virus, Spybot and AVG.

PAY PROTECTION

Over the years, in general I have preferred Norton; however, it's best to read up on the current reviews for protection if planning to purchase one.

HOW WE PERFORM VIRUS REMOVAL

Listed below is how our techs attempt to remove a virus. We use the word "attempt" because we never know whether or not we are successful until we run every removal program and then test the computer on the Internet. If these steps are followed and the computer still doesn't work properly, re-install Windows.

1. If possible, attempt to boot the computer into SAFE MODE. Use the "Shift + Restart" combination. Another way of getting into Safe Mode in Windows is to use the Shift + Restart combination. With older computes, press F8 on startup and select SAFE MODE WITH NETWORKING.
2. If the computer loads into Windows, run RKILL first, then manually update and run the other protection programs on the computer.
3. Reset the web browser.
4. Manually run the other protection programs – ADW Cleaner, Junkware Removal Tool, Malwarebytes, and Superantispyware. Get updates on each program prior to running.
5. Update and run anti-virus software.
6. If the computer works, Windows updates will be downloaded and installed.
7. Manually check for Windows updates.
8. Optimize the system.
9. The computer will be tested both on and off the Internet.

ONLINE VIRUS SCANNERS

This sample screen is from ESET ONLINE SCANNER, which at this time of this writing is one of the best free online scanners on the market. If the computer works online, search for "Eset online scanner" and follow the link for scanning the computer.

When using Eset or any other online scanner check the default settings and <u>change them if necessary to scan AND REMOVE any viruses found</u>. Eset scanner may be set to scan only and not to remove any viruses found.

To check for other online scanners, search for "free online virus scanners" and see what shows up. Be aware that free online virus scanners, like all free stuff on the internet may be placing tracking cookies on a computer. Nothing is truly free.

SMART PHONE VIRUSES

Smart phone can get viruses. Phone viruses began in 2004.In August 2010, Kaspersky Lab reported the first malicious program named Trojan-SMS. At present, they can't spread very far and they don't do much damage, but the future might see cell-phone bugs that are as debilitating as computer viruses.

Infected files can show up disguised as applications like games, security patches, pornography and free downloads. Infected text messages sometimes steal the subject line from a message received from a friend, which increases the likelihood of it being opened -- but opening the message may not be enough to get infected.

PHONE VIRUS REMOVAL

Discuss phone viruses with the phone's wireless provider and check the wireless provider and phone manufacturer website for information. Resetting the phone should remove the virus; however, you lose all information and have to re-program the phone.

TABLETS AND VIRUSES

Reset any virus on an Android tablet. To RESET, enter the SYSTEM settings and RESET BACK TO FACTORY. If the Tablet is Windows-based and the information is important, attempt the virus removal steps issued earlier. If the data is not important, RESET the tablet.

VISHING AND SMISHING

These are common terms for people sending either voice mails or text messages directly to a smart phone telling saying that your account has been compromised and to respond with personal information for verification of account.

Don't do it. If the message seems legitimate, call someone on a phone to verify that your account has been compromised.

USE COMMON SENSE

The best protection against viruses and spyware is to use good common sense. Most people wouldn't walk alone down a deserted city block late at night. Don't accept any contact from any email that initiates the contact. Refrain from clicking on ads, especially ads on social media.

IS THERE ANY FULLPROOF METHOD TO NOT GET VIRUSES AND SPYWARE?

Don't use the Internet, period. For most people, this is not a viable option. If you plan to use the Internet, be prepared to deal with viruses, spyware, malware, hijackers, and junk files. It doesn't matter how careful you are, you're going to get stuff on a computer.

Viruses, spyware and malware are a fact of computer life. You WILL get junk on your computer. The best virus protection is to use common sense and avoid getting them.

21. ONLINE & SOCIAL NETWORKING

A social network is defined as a social structure made up of individuals or organizations called "nodes", which are connected by one or more specific types of interdependency, such as friendship, common interest, and financial exchange, sexual or other type of relationship.

Over TWO BILLION people use Facebook. People also use Twitter, Instagram, Pinterest, Match, YouTube, chat rooms and many websites for meeting and interacting with others. The Internet is the most popular meeting place to interact with people.

Remember that while interacting with others online can be fun; however, be aware of exposing personal information to others. Those that use social networking sites to keep access to your private information to a minimum consider the following:

VIRUSES, SPYWARE AND MALWARE

Online sites are a collection point for viruses, spyware and malware. Usually problems will be picked up by clicking on the advertisements placed on the sites.

SOCIAL NETWORKING SCAMS

Many online scammers attempt to solicit money or information through social networks. The scam begins when the user receives a message like this "ha-ha did you see this yet? It's pretty funny". Clicking on the link of that type could unknowingly forward this message to all contacts on the computer or it could collect information.

FACEBOOK PROTECTION TIPS

Since Facebook is the largest used social network site, we thought it appropriate to base protection tips for their site. These tips can be applied on other sites.

1. DISABLE PLACES

Places are suggested links to visit. If using Facebook Places remember that by default all user information is exposed. Your information is exposed to others. Some viewers may not have good intentions. Select ACCOUNT TAB and PRIVACY SETTINGS to adjust and secure the profile.

2. DISABLE FACEBOOK APPS

Select PRIVACY SETTINGS / TURN OFF ALL PLATFORM APPS.

3. DON'T PICK FRIENDS ARBITRARILY

There is no reason to "Friend" a stranger because Facebook recommends someone.

4. CONTROL POSTINGS

Control your post views and access to them by using the LOCK feature. Prior to clicking on SHARE, click the drop-down menu above and select who can see the post: The last setting should let a user block individual friends no matter who you select for viewing.

5. HIDE APP ACTIVITY

Hide the fact that you play games on Facebook and all Facebook activity by selecting: Under PRIVACY / APPLICATIONS & WEBSITES / EDIT YOUR SETTINGS / GAMES AND APPLICATIONS ACTIVITY / CUSTOM / ONLY ME.

6. CONTROL WHAT FRIENDS REVEAL

To reduce friend's access to your account: PRIVACY SETTINGS / APPLICATIONS AND WEBSITES / EDIT YOUR SETTINGS / INFO ACCESSABLE THROUGH YOUR FRIENDS. Deselect items to share profile information with friends.

7. DELETE THE ACCOUNT

To actually delete the account, access Face book's Help Pages and fill out a submission form, otherwise DEACTIVATE the account, which doesn't remove it.

FACEBOOK HACKS

Facebook had multiple hacks into their data. If you use Facebook do not give them any data such as social security number, address or phone number if possible.

TWITTER

Twitter is a website which offers a social networking and micro blogging service, enabling its users to send and read short messages called tweets. Twitter has gained popularity worldwide and is estimated to have 200 million users, generating 200 million tweets a day and handling over 1.6 billion search queries per day.

Tweets are publicly visible by default; however, senders can restrict message delivery to just their followers. Users can tweet via the Twitter website or by any Internet capable device such as a smartphone or I pad.

Users may subscribe to other member tweets – this is known as following and subscribers are known as followers. Twitter allows users the ability to update their profile by using their mobile phone either by text messaging or by apps released for certain smartphones or tablets.

As a social network, Twitter revolves on the principle of followers. If a person likes your "Tweets" they will sign up as a follower on your Twitter page. The tweets appear in reverse chronological order on the user's main Twitter page.

Twitter will display the tweets of the people you are following. If you follow 20 people, you'll see a mix of tweets scrolling down the page: breakfast-cereal updates, interesting new links, music recommendations and other things.

TWITTER ISSUES

Twitter tends to be less problematic as a social networking site because most of the time people are simply viewing tweets. The biggest problem with Twitter is that the Twitter site tends to get overloaded with users and there can be delays accessing the site. Realize that many people are self-promoting either their product or service and want you to check out their site. Be careful. Just because someone's on Twitter doesn't mean that they're legit.

INSTAGRAM AND PINTEREST

Instagram and Pinterest are social media sites that focus on users sharing photographs or interests. These sites, just like Facebook and Twitter can act as carriers for passing on viruses, spyware and malware to your computer or phone.

PHISHING SITES

A phishing site is any website created for the sole purpose of grabbing information from the visitor. The bad guys are the fisherman and they are "fishing" for information. They are hoping to collect private sensitive information to either sell or use it to turn an illegal profit. A fish is "caught" on the hook when they give the fisherman personal information through a website or email that was mistaken as a legitimate site.

A phishing site could resemble a bank, mortgage or any legitimate site normally visited. A phishing email is soliciting information. Possibly an unsolicited email requesting updated information. It may ask for checking account, credit card information or social security number. DON'T GIVE IT. If you suspect the request is fraudulent, delete the email and CALL the company using a phone number from the company website to verify the information request.

THINGS TO AVOID

Be careful if you get approached online by any of the following:

- Any POPUP that states there is spyware on the computer and CLICK HERE to remove the spyware.
- Any email that has spelling errors or poor grammar.
- A picture of a pretty girl that says she is lonely and wants to meet you. CLICK HERE to email me.
- Any email claims you just won a prize. CLICK HERE to redeem your prize.

- An email or popup claims there is a problem with:

  1. Bank account
  2. EBay account.
  3. Credit card account
  4. Other account of importance

They ask you to click on a link to correct problem. Never click on any link in an email. If you believe the request may be legitimate, Again, PICK UP THE PHONE AND CALL to verify.

SECURITY SUITES

It's no longer enough to have antivirus software to scan and remove viruses from a PC. Some protection programs will verify whether a pop-up or link is legitimate, if a website is safe or whether that site is just attempting to gather sensitive financial information.

An Internet Security Suite is a set of software and services that helps protect a computer from hackers, viruses, spyware, and other threats. Security Suites are automatically updated to keep the user protected from new threats online.

POPULAR SECURITY SUITES

- Kaspersky Total Security
- Bitdefender Total Security
- Norton Security Premium
- Trend Micro Maximum Security
- F-Secure Safe
- McAfee Total Protection
- ESET Smart Security Premium
- Panda Global Protection

Remember that this list as of the date of this writing and is subject to change.

THE PROBLEM WITH SECURITY SUITES

Security suites slow up any system. Security suites have to process more information than virus software and require more system resources. Make sure to have enough memory, processing speed and storage space. Don't compound the problem by having multiple viruses, spyware or malware programs running on a system.

INFORMATION PROTECTION PROGRAMS

Companies such as Life lock advertise that they monitor user personal information online and assist if user information gets compromised. Be careful and use common sense when providing personal information online and never pay with a bank debit card.

HOW CAN I KNOW WHETHER AN UNKNOWN WEBSITE IS SAFE?

Download and install the Web of Trust (mywot.com). This is a free browser plug-in that's available for Explorer, Firefox, Chrome and Safari. This useful tool searches results prior to selecting the site. Web of Trust uses a car traffic light rating system (red, yellow, and green) to indicate which links to avoid and which are safe.

PROTECT YOURSELF

1. **DON'T OPEN EMAIL ATTACHMENTS**

   Some banks or other businesses may send emails stating that your monthly statement is online. Unless the link is from the institution, log in independently to the bank site. Don't click on the email attachment.

2. **DON'T LOG ONTO A NON-SECURE PAGE**

   Don't log onto any website beginning with HTTP. Verify the IP address states HTTPS.

3. **USE A GOOD PASSWORD**

   A password like j8A5s9kul1$ski is a good password. It mixes letters, numbers and case sensitivity. Review the PASSWORD section for other ideas.

4. **AVOID PUBLIC NETWORKS**
   Don't log into a bank or other financial site from an Internet café or open wireless network. Log in only at work or home.

INVASIVE PROGRAMS

An invasive program (Also referred to as a PUP-Potentially Unwanted Program) is any program that unnecessarily draws resource from a system. There are different types of invasive programs:

JUNK PROGRAMS

We discussed earlier that computer manufacturers get reimbursed by software companies for distributing their programs. Computer manufacturers get paid from software companies by installing third party software on their computers prior to shipping. The computer acts as a distributor for all these programs.

NEW COMPUTERS

Computer manufacturers are paid by the junk program developers to install their programs on the computer prior to shipping. The first thing to do with a brand new computer out of the box is to enter CONTROL PANEL / PROGRAMS and Select ADD REMOVE PROGRAMS to uninstall all junk programs that will not be used. If you aren't sure a program is considered junk, do not uninstall it until the program is researched.

Clean up and update the computer prior to making a backup image or set of recovery DVDs so this process only has to be done one time. If the recovery DVDs is made first, the system will have to be cleaned and updated again if the recovery media has to be used to re-install Windows.

PROGRAMS LOADING UNNECESSARILY ON STARTUP

Many programs that load during startup when the computer is turned on can be considered invasive. Why should every program on the computer load into memory if they won't be used? Why take up the resource?

If only plan to access the Internet, there is no reason for programs like QuickBooks, Microsoft Office, Windows Media Player, or the up to 50 other programs that are loading each time the computer is turned on.

Invasive programs can be found under the SERVICES option. Whether the program is providing a service is open to debate; however, it's still a program, loading each time the computer is turned on. Turn off all non-Microsoft and non-essential programs.

WHAT IS ESSENTIAL AND WHAT'S NOT?

Turn off non-essential programs in STARTUP and all non-essential Microsoft Programs in SERVICES and restart the computer. Play a movie and attempt to get onto the Internet and play something with sound, both connected and wirelessly. If both processes work, do not turn off anything else to load into startup except anti-virus and system security programs. The computer will operate faster on start-up and running with fewer programs loading into memory when the computer is turned on.

WHAT IS IMPORTANT AND NOT TO TURN OFF?

Usually anything that the system requires be on will be turned back on automatically; however, to be safe, either research a process online or leave any process on if unsure of its function.

TRIAL SOFTWARE

Trial software is software that will shut down in 30 days unless it's purchased. Uninstall or disable all trial programs installed on new computers and replace them with permanent freeware programs. We have had many complaints over the years from customers that used a trial program and had the program shut down on them.

PROGRAMS THAT WON'T UNINSTALL

Certain programs may not install easily. They purposely make their programs hard to uninstall from a system. These programs may require an uninstall program in order to remove it from a computer. Check online or at the software's website for such a program

WEB BROWSER TOOLBARS

Web toolbars may be placed on a system either legitimately by a company or by spyware. Freeware, shareware and commercial applications sometimes attempt to install a web toolbar on a system during installation of their program. The largest offenders of forcing their web toolbar are Google, Yahoo, Adobe and Microsoft. Web companies have reciprocal agreements and pay each other for referrals or download of their software.

A user may go to Adobe's website to download Adobe Flash or Reader. Adobe Flash and Adobe Reader are good free downloads to have on a computer.

Adobe may offer a free download of McAfee or Google Chrome at their site. Usually the program being offered is already checked, assuming that the site visitor wishes the download. Be careful when downloading a program or update not to receive an additional "bonus" in the form of another program.

Check PROGRAMS or ADD / REMOVE PROGRAMS to uninstall any toolbar or other unnecessary program. If the program isn't listed under Programs, it could be spyware or malware. In that case, run a spyware and malware removal tool to remove it.

Online travels are fraught with all types of possible issues for a computer. Be careful because it's a jungle out there.

22. PASSWORDS

Passwords are used every day to gain access to something. We password everything from our garage door and home alarm systems to the car, gym locker and even the shed door that houses nothing but junk. Computer and online passwords provide access to everything from our bank accounts to every website we've made a purchase.

COMPUTER PASSWORDS

Computer passwords are supposed to keep other people from accessing important files; however, passwords can create problems as well. When deciding whether or not to use a password on a computer to prevent computer access from unauthorized people:

- Passwords are easy to forget.
- Passwords can be changed.
- Passwords can come back to haunt you.

PASSWORDS ARE EASY TO FORGET

Write a password down somewhere. Don't rely on memory. There's a problem if that password is forgotten. Most websites have a link that says "Forgot Password" so in many cases a password can be recovered; however why have to go through that process in the first place? There isn't such a link for the password on your Windows computer other than a "Hint" option that most people don't fill out. Write down the password.

PASSWORDS CAN BE CHANGED

Anyone that has access to the system and passwords can log into the USER account and change a password without permission. If they have that kind of access, why is the computer being pass-worded in the first place?

PERMISSIONED DATA

Permissioned data is data that cannot be retrieved because the hard drive was pulled from the computer and the data on the drive is not accessible without removing the prior password security. The original password setup on that account may remain in place and makes the data not retrievable. Permissions are discussed in detail under the Data Save section.

SYSTEM versus WINDOWS PASSWORD

There are two types of computer passwords – System passwords and Windows passwords. Both require a password to gain access; however, one can cause a much greater problem if forgotten.

THE SYSTEM or BIOS PASSWORD

PCs have the capability for a user to setup a system password. The system password is a feature provided in the Setup utility program. The system password must be entered PRIOR to starting Windows.

HOW TO SETUP A SYSTEM PASSWORD

A System password must be configured in the System program. The Setup program is accessed by pressing the DELETE, F1 or F2 keys when turning on the computer. The computer should list on the screen at initial boot up which key to press to access Setup

A solid blue or black setup screen will appear. Search under the ADVANCED menu to find the password setup option. Once set, the system password must be entered prior to starting Windows.

Most passwords are upper and lower case sensitive. Some systems allow the usage of characters. A system password is more difficult to remove than a Windows password, so don't set a complex password using a system password.

SYSTEM PASSWORDS ARE DANGEROUS

If a system password doesn't work, a computer store may have to get the non-working password removed. In some cases, to remove a System passwords, the computer motherboard battery must be removed, which means taking apart the computer.

Removing the battery from the motherboard drains the battery. When the battery is drained, all settings being held in the battery are lost, including the password. The default system settings can be reset on the system once the battery is replaced.

A notebook system password is difficult to remove, because a notebook takes much longer to take apart to get to the battery for removal. Contact the computer manufacturer to see if there is a workaround for a system password removal.

WINDOWS PASSWORD

Windows permit single or multiple users to password their accounts. Each user on the computer can have some semblance of privacy by pass wording. Passwords can be setup under USERS in Control Panel. If a password must be used, a Windows password is easier to remove than a System password in the event of a password problem.

THE ADMINISTRATOR

A separate administrator account can be setup on a Windows based PC. The administrator has privileges that override the other users. The administrator can control every aspect of the system, including the removal of passwords of the other users.

RESET A PASSWORD

1. Start the PC and select the Power icon in the bottom right-hand corner of the lock screen.
2. While holding down the Shift key, select RESTART.
3. On the Boot options menu, select TROUBLESHOOT / RESET THIS PC and REMOVE EVERYTHING.
4. The PC will restart and will reset itself. Programs will have to be reinstalled.

REMOVE A WINDOWS PASSWORD

A Windows password can be removed under the USER account in Control Panel. Under CONTROL PANEL / USERS, turn off the password. If a Windows password doesn't work and cannot be removed, the following approaches for removal:

1. **REMOVE A PASSWORD IN SAFE MODE**

    To remove a password attempt to startup in Safe Mode and attempt to access the administrator account. The problem may still exist in SAFE MODE. If the password cannot be removed in Safe Mode:

    - Create a new user account.
    - Give the new user administrative privileges.
    - Restart the computer and attempt to remove all User accounts using the new user account that has administrative privileges.

2. **RESTORE POINT**

    If possible, use a restore point to revert back in time prior to the password problem.

3. **PASSWORD REMOVAL PROGRAM**

    Download a Windows password removal program. Perform a Google search on password removal tools. Download and run the free programs first.

4. **RE-INSTALL WINDOWS**

    Format the hard drive and re-install Windows. Resetting the computer will take less time, remove the password and all data will be removed.

ONLINE PASSWORDS

Most websites attempt to get a visitor to setup an account at the site. Online accounts require a LOGIN or USER ID and PASSWORD. Take precautions when setting up passwords:

CREATE PASSWORD DIFFICULT TO HACK

Passwords should be well thought out and not something simple, like a child's' name or birthdates. A good password would be something like KMJ15A6 or ALab41P4T.

Bankcard pin codes are more difficult to protect because pin codes are numeric only. Use a non-birthdates or graduation date number. A professional identity thief has methods to get that type of basic information. Don't make it easy for the crooks.

MIX UP PASSWORDS

Don't use the same online password for every site. Use difficult passwords for banking, mortgage, broker or other important sites where security is critical. Consider using a different password for email access, Facebook or any other lower priority website. There is a better chance that a social networking site would get hacked.

CHANGE PASSWORD PERIODICALLY

Change passwords periodically. Do not use the same passwords on every website.

PASSWORD STORAGE – WRITE THEM DOWN

I have a book of Login or User Account and Passwords that is at least 15 pages thick. Every password change I make is placed in the book. If that book ever gets lost or stolen, I'm sunk; however, I prefer this method instead of keeping password on a computer.

Password storage can be done by keeping all passwords in a password storing program or in an online cloud program. When it comes to passwords, I prefer the old school method. I keep them in a book. What happens if the passwords get stolen or gain access online?

ONLINE OR PROGRAM PASSWORD TOOLS

There are programs and sites that allow online password storage online. A possible issue with using a computer password program is what happens if the computer crashes? Who else has access to passwords if they are stored online? Any system can be hacked.

Write down passwords, make passwords difficult to hack and change them at least once a year.

23. DEVICE DRIVERS

A driver in computer terms is special software for a part or device that is installed in the computer. A device driver is software that interfaces a hardware device with Windows. Device driver software acts as a traffic cop so that the computer hardware device can co-exist with Windows. Driver software is necessary with the following parts:

- CPU and onboard devices
- Video card
- Network card
- Wireless network card
- Wireless mice and keyboard
- Soundcard
- The mouse, keyboard, optical drive, USB ports, etc.
-

WINDOWS DRIVERS AND MANUFACTURER DRIVERS

Windows has its own database of drivers and will automatically install the driver that it feels is the best choice for that particular device. It may or may not be the driver provided by the manufacturer of the hardware. Most of the time Windows gets it right; however, on occasion Windows may install the wrong driver.

When Windows misses, it's mostly with the video driver, which causes the most problems with the computer. Normally mice and keyboard drivers won't have to be installed. Windows drivers will install most physically connected mice and keyboards.

This is a sample screen of DEVICE MANAGER. Check this screen to see if Windows correctly recognizes all the device drivers. Any problem driver will have a question mark or exclamation point next to the problem device.

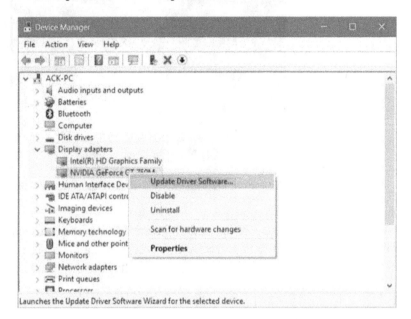

WHERE DO I GET DRIVERS?

Hardware manufacturers provide drivers at their websites for downloading. When purchased, a driver DVD is usually provided. Other websites may provide device drivers; however, make sure that the website is not charging for downloading drivers to a computer.

DRIVER UPDATER PROGRAMS

There are programs that will automatically update computer system device drivers; however, some of these programs will also download other junk programs onto a computer which is how they make their money. I prefer to just let Windows get the driver updates. Windows may not get the very latest driver updates; however, many outdated drivers should be updated automatically with less risk of getting other junk programs downloaded on the computer.

HOW DO I KNOW IF THERE IS A DRIVER PROBLEM?

Most people will not; however, updating a device driver is something to attempt to fix a problem. If the sound isn't working, the video isn't correct or another device issue, first update the device driver.

HOW TO REPAIR A DRIVER PROBLEM

1. DISCONNECT ANY NEW HARDWARE

If new hardware was installed, the necessary driver for that hardware might not be installed, or the driver might be incompatible or corrupted. To determine whether this is true, follow these steps:
- Disconnect the device or remove the device from the system.
- Restart Windows.
- If Windows starts successfully, there is a driver issue with the new hardware. Contact the device manufacturer or re-download the device driver from the manufacturer's website.

2. UPDATE THE DRIVER

Enter DEVICE MANAGER, right click on the driver not working properly and select UPDATE DRIVER. Windows will automatically search online and attempt to find the correct driver for the device.

3. USE THE LAST KNOWN GOOD CONFIGURATION FEATURE

If the computer starts, select the LAST KNOWN GOOD CONFIGURATION option under SAFE MODE. This feature will restore Windows back to when the system was last working correctly. Use this feature to restore registry settings and drivers back to their previous configuration.

First boot up into Safe Mode or use the Repair Option. With older computers, press the F8 key repeatedly until the Advanced Options screen in Safe Mode is displayed. Use the arrow keys to select Last Known Good Configuration (the most recent settings that worked), and press ENTER.

4. ROLLBACK THE DRIVER

On occasion a Windows update may include a hardware driver update for a computer and that driver. Under DEVICE MANAGER, find the device with the problem and attempt to ROLL BACK the driver.

A roll back installs a previous driver for the device selected to roll back. To Roll Back a driver, enter DEVICE MANAGER and Right Click on the Device and enter PROPERTIES. Roll back the driver at that point.

5. DELETE THE DRIVER

Delete the device from Device Manager and re-install the driver from the manufacturer CD or download. Windows should attempt to re-install the driver from within the Windows database of device drivers. If Windows cannot find the correct driver, the system will prompt to find correct driver on the Internet.

GOOGLE THE DRIVER

GOOGLE the make and model followed by "DRIVER DOWNLOAD" Example: "Sony PCG-5139 Driver. A list of sites with that driver should appear. Be careful about the site selected. Many sites will want to charge for the driver.

Corrupt or missing drivers can cause problems. Check DEVICE MANAGER to verify that the devices are working properly.

24. PLUGINS & ADD-ONS

A plug-in or Add-on is a software upgrade that adds capability to a larger software application. Plugins are used in web browsers to play video, scan for viruses, and display new file types. Popular Plugins:

ADOBE FLASH

Adobe Flash is required by some websites to play videos on a computer. Flash is required to play YouTube and Facebook videos. Windows usually will automatically apply any necessary Adobe updates.

ADOBE FREE DOWNLOADS

Adobe offers some of the more popular add on programs. Adobe offers free downloads of their programs on their website, including Adobe Reader, which reads PDF Files. Adobe Flash is a free download and can be found at Adobe's website, adobe.com. Many sites that require Flash may automatically prompt for the Flash download.

BROWSER PLUGINS AND ADD ONS

Web browser add-ons will add extra features and functionality to web browsers (for example, extra toolbars, animated mouse pointers, stock tickers, and pop-up (ad blockers) enhance the web browser.

Many add-ons and Plugins will attempt to attach themselves to the Internet Browser. Some Plugins can be helpful. The best place to search for and retrieve web browser add-ons would be at the web browser online store. For Microsoft products use the Microsoft store and for Google Chrome use the Google Chrome store.

PUP AND JUNK ADD ONS

While some add-ons are beneficial, others would be considered junk or PUPs (Potentially Unwanted Programs). They can get attached inside a web browser. If unsure what a program on the Internet browser is doing, look to uninstall the program under DEVICE MANAGER / PROGRAMS.

CODEC

A valuable plug-in is a codec. A codec is a device or computer program capable of encoding and/or decoding a digital data stream or signal. A codec encodes a data stream or signal for transmission, storage or encryption, or decodes it for playback or editing. Codecs are used in videoconferencing, streaming media and video editing applications and to play movies. An online movie or movie on DVD cannot play on a computer without a codec.

Windows will usually handle the playing of a movie without any problem. If a movie doesn't play a movie on media player, attempt to download a free codec from the Internet. Google "Free Codec Download" and see what's available

BE CAREFUL

Junkware can be placed on a computer in the form of browser add-ons and tool bars. Usually they get installed along with a program that the user downloaded to the system.

WHERE TO ACQUIRE BROWSER BASED ADD-ON PROGRAMS

Check the Microsoft Store for Edge and Explorer add-ons and the Chrome store for Chrome add-ons.

Add-Ons and Plugins can be useful but verify them as legitimate before installing.

25. OTHER TYPE REPAIRS

Listed below are other types of repairs that may help when working on a computer.

1. CD STUCK IN THE CD OPTICAL DRIVE

A CD stuck in a CD drive that won't open can be removed by forcing a paper clip into a small pinhole on the bottom right of the CD under the eject button. The pinhole acts as an emergency eject button. Insert the straightened paper clip until there is resistance and the CD drawer should force the CD drive to pop open.

2. CHKDSK REPAIR

If Windows will not start, attempt to repair Windows by running a Check Disk Repair. A Windows Chkdsk or Scandisk repair will check the computer hard drive and check each hard drive sector. It will attempt to repair any irregularities on the hard drive and Windows files if possible. This process may correct Windows at least well enough so files can be retrieved.

A Windows Check Disk Repair doesn't remove any viruses or spyware. These are separate processes that need to be run. Since Windows doesn't work, a Check Disk Repair needs to be run off a bootable CD or flash drive. Bootable means that the computer will start when accessing that particular device.

If a Windows Recovery USB or CD is bootable; the computer can start from that device or CD and run a program, in this case a Windows re-installation program. Any bootable program has the ability to run on its own once started.

Good programs to download are ACTIVE BOOT DISK and HIRENS. Look into the AVAST or BART CD with the Chkdsk repair program. A Windows boot disk may run the similar program.

3. RESEAT ALL CARDS AND MEMORY

Sometimes just reseating the cards and memory in a desktop or notebook corrects a problem.

4. RESTORE POINTS

One easy method to repair a Windows problem is to select a Restore Point or run Last Known Good Configuration in Safe Mode. Assuming the computer will boot into Windows, to run a restore point select / CONTROL PANEL / RECOVERY / OPEN SYSTEM RESTORE / Select a RESTORE POINT.

5. REMOVE THE DESKTOP POWER PLUG AND RECONNECT FIRMLY

On occasion a minor surge hit may only "lock" a power supply and not blow it. If the computer isn't powering on, remove the power cord and reconnect it FIRMLY. Really push it in. Sometimes re-plugging the power cord resets the power supply and it corrects the startup problem.

6. SMALLER DRIVE NOTEBOOKS – RUN DISK CLEANUP MULTIPLE TIMES

When working on a smaller netbook with only a 32 or 64 gig SSD drive for storage, run the DISK CLEANUP utility multiple times and make sure to select CLEAN SYSTEM FILES when running Disk Cleanup the second time or last time. Make sure to select "Prior Windows Versions" to remove. That will remove any prior Windows installations and should free up a significant amount of hard drive space. On the smaller netbooks with tiny sized drives, every gigabyte matters.

Review these repairs when in trouble.

26. REPAIR, UPGRADE or REPLACE?

Many customers question whether to repair or replace when their computer needs repair work and they're going to have to spend money. Some advice to help making the decision:

REPLACE

If the computer needs to be repaired and is licensed with a Windows version older than Windows 7, replace it. This includes any computer licensed with Windows Vista, Windows 95, Windows 98, Millennium and Windows 2000.

Replace any computer if repairing the computer is going to cost over 50% of replacing it with a new computer.

REPAIR

If the repair is software related or a minor hardware problem and the repair is $100 or less, get it repaired. A repair over $150, consider replacing the system as an option.

WHEN REPLACING

When replacing a computer, <u>never</u> go backwards on computing hardware CPU power and storage. The cost per gigahertz and gigabyte per dollar spent is as inexpensive as ever. Don't even stay even with a minor upgrade. Don't cheat yourself.

Let's assume a notebook hard drive failed and needs to be replaced. The service department quotes a price of $200. The first reaction is that for $200 it's better to just replace the notebook with a newer model.

REPLACE A USED MERCEDES WITH A NEW YUGO?

Before committing, find out what $200 will include if purchasing a new computer. Is it a netbook that has a smaller screen, keyboard and no optical drive? The lower price pointed desktops and notebooks aren't made as well and use low-priced components.

New doesn't mean well made. Less expensive equipment generally uses slower processors and may have additional repair issues. Don't be swayed just because a computer is new. Check the system specifications and read reviews.

DIAGNOSTIC COST

How much will it cost for a diagnostic? Will the diagnostic fee apply towards a replacement when after the diagnostic is completed? What happens if you don't want to have the work done? The user is out the upfront diagnostic fee if they decide not to have the system repaired.

DON'T FACTOR A DATA SAVE INTO A DECISION

If the computer repair requires a data save, don't factor that into a decision to repair or replace the computer. If the data is important, a data save is required whether the computer is repaired or replaced. Ask the service center if they will transfer files from an old computer free if a new computer is purchased from them.

SHOULD I UPGRADE MY OLD SYSTEM?

Yes, if the upgrade is adding additional memory only. Don't upgrade other parts. Forget about attempting to add a faster processor, larger hard drive or upgrading Windows. Those upgrades typically aren't worth the dollar and headache cost.

MEMORY

Why is upgrading memory the most effective upgrade? This example may help understand why having enough computer memory is important:

Imagine a residence with a fenced- in backyard. A party is being planned, using the back yard to have an outside party for the neighborhood. The food and refreshments are setup on a table farthest away from the house at the back far corner of the yard. It's early and the party hasn't started yet. To walk from the back of the house to grab a beer from a cooler at the farthest part in the back yard takes 20 seconds.

Now it's two hours later and the party is crowded. Your teenagers decided to invite their friends and now there is three times the number of people in attendance all crammed in your fenced-in back yard. Now that same walk from the house to grab a beer takes over a minute because now the back yard is crowded and to get to that beer requires navigating through a crowd.

Imagine computer memory as the available square footage area in the fenced-in yard. Each person in the yard is each individual program loading into the computer memory when the computer is turned on. Adding additional memory in the system is similar to expanding the backyard area so the people can spread out, making it easier to navigate to the food. Additional memory can provide more space for programs to run so the programs work faster.

DRIVE SPACE

Hard drive space is permanent storage on a computer. Data stored on the hard drive remains there unless it's removed. If a hard drive is over 70% filled, purchase an external hard drive. Move all movies, music and photos off the computer to the external.

Another option is to purchase a larger hard drive and have a computer shop "Image" or duplicate the entire hard drive contents onto the larger drive and replace the larger drive back in the computer. Let the computer shop handle hard drive imaging. Larger flash drives are less expensive and an easy way to add more drive space.

Avoid purchasing any new netbook with only a 32 gig SSD drive for storage. Purchase any lower cost notebook with at least a 64 gig SSD drive as a minimum drive storage capacity. The 32 gig units are too easy to fill up completely and once that happens, the unit is not usable. It may have to be taken to a shop for repair, unless the user has a bootable USB Windows installation media device.

CPU

The motherboard determines the CPU system processing and upgrading capabilities. Research the motherboard specifications and capabilities to determine if the computer will accept a faster CPU. Most CPU upgrades won't increase the speed enough to be worth the cost.

Many computers no longer ship with manuals. Refer to the manufacturer's website for any technical information on your computer. If upgrading, be careful when removing the old and replacing the new CPU. Many a tech has fried processors and motherboard alike by installing a CPU chip incorrectly.

VIDEO

Video upgrades can only be performed on desktop computers, not laptops or notebooks. Video cards on laptops and notebooks are soldered to the main processing board and not upgradeable affordably.

A video card upgrade may be advised for gamers or an online movie or video watcher. On-board integrated video cards are very good but won't process as quickly as a separate video card in a system.

A separate video card will increase video performance because the video card handles the graphics processing that previously the motherboard had to handle. The distributive processing frees up motherboard resource and the graphics look better and work faster

Purchase a video card with as much memory on the card as possible. Notebooks may advertise a high end video card with their system specifications; however, they still have a motherboard and processor bottleneck when processing video and graphics.

BIOS

The CMOS or BIOS is a firmware upgrade provided by the manufacturer.
Avoid BIOS upgrades unless you're attempting to repair a specific problem that according to research a bios upgrade will correct. Be sure to create a new Restore Point and backup all important data prior to a bios upgrade.

Consider a repair if the repair costs up to $150 or if the system repair is at least 50% less than replacing it.

27. DATA RECOVERY FROM A BROKEN COMPUTER

AFTER CRUCIAL INFORMATION WAS INADVERTENTLY ERASED, EXPERTS WERE CALLED IN TO PERFORM DATA RECOVERY

We hear this at least once a week:

- "My computer died and I can't get to my data."
- "Windows won't start and I need my data."
- "My teen was on Facebook and my computer's screwed up and my data isn't backed up".
- "I can't get my data off this old computer".
- "I just bought a new computer and want my data transferred to my new computer".

It is always about the data. People want those kiddie photos, those ITunes, that proposal, that resume, something on that broken computer is very important. If the computer was working or the data was backed up the data, they wouldn't be in my shop; however, the computer doesn't work and the data isn't backed up, so let's deal with the problem.

SAVING DATA FROM A WORKING COMPUTER

Move the data off the computer onto an external backup. If the computer doesn't start Windows, attempt to start Windows in Windows SAFE MODE. If the system works, copy the data off the drive, re-install the programs on the replacement computer and then restore the data. The computer isn't working; however, so let's move forward.

SAVING DATA FROM A NON-WORKING COMPUTER

There are three methods to move information from a non-working computer to gain access to the information on the hard drive – electronically transfer the data, mount the hard drive in different computer to read the drive and pull data or mount the hard drive in an external case enclosure and use as an external storage device. We are assuming in all three examples that the hard drive hasn't failed and the data on the drive is retrievable.

1. ELECTRONICALLY TRANSER THE DATA

Method One is to transfer data is electronically transfer files from the non-working computer. This method assumes the computer powers on but will not start Windows even in Safe Mode.

Use a bootable flash drive and load the Active Boot Disk or other program that has a file transfer utility. If there is a lot of data to transfer, connect an external hard drive with enough storage space. Run the file transfer program off the bootable CD or flash drive to get the files off the non-working system.

Transferring data is not transferring the programs.

Microsoft Office, TurboTax, QuickBooks and other non-Windows programs will have to be re-downloaded or re-installed from original CDs. If the USERS folder and its contents is saved and placed on a new computer, the letters, spreadsheets and all information stored there should be accessible.

Microsoft Office (Word, Excel, and the OFFICE programs) is NOT part of Windows.

If files are saved, do not assume Microsoft Office will be usable when accessing saved or recovered data on a replacement computer.

2. MOUNT THE OLD HARD DRIVE IN A DIFFERENT COMPUTER

A second method to get data from the old computer is to mount the old hard drive from the non-working computer into a different system. Windows will display the new drive as a slave drive in MY PC (letter D or lower). Once connected, the drive can be used as a separate storage area.

The advantage of this option is that the data on this drive shouldn't be affected if Windows crashes on the main (C) drive. Transferring of data will be faster because data will be transferred drive to drive and not through a USB connection.

It's probably not a good idea to install the old drive into the new computer. A potential problem is that the hard drive may conflict with the existing hard drive in the system. If Windows doesn't work, the data drive won't be accessible.

Even if there isn't a drive conflict, suppose the system crashes? The backup data on that drive won't be accessible because the drive is installed in a system that doesn't work.

3. MOUNT THE OLD HARD DRIVE IN A CASE ENCLOSURE

The original hard drive is removed from the non-working computer and placed in an external hard drive case enclosure, pictured below.

If the computer isn't affordably repairable, select this option because all the data will be available. There is no 100% guarantee that every email, file and document will be transferred using Method One – the electronic transfer method. All the data should be available because the original drive is being accessed.

Be careful going forward using an older drive as the primary storage for backup. Remember the drive is older and more likely to fail.

PERMISSIONED DATA

A possible problem with any data save can occur with what is called Permissioned Data. Permissioned data is data on a hard drive that is not accessible. Permissioned data happens when a hard drive is removed from a computer for a data transfer and the original user or users pass worded their Windows accounts on the drive to be read.

Data is permissioned on a hard drive when either the folders are blank or when attempting to access a folder, the system will respond with a prompt "Access Denied". The permissions must be removed from the hard drive to get to the data.

Windows still believes the user account protection is still in effect proper even though the hard drive is no longer in the computer. As far as Windows is concerned, proper access needs to be gained to get access to the data.

To remove data permissions so the data can be accessed:

1. Usually just connecting the hard drive to a Windows 7 or later system and accessing the data will automatically remove the prior permissions on the hard drive. The process may take a while so be patient.
2. Google "Hard drive permission removal programs."
3. The drive must be hooked up as a slave and ownership must be taken of that drive. Google how to do this.
4. Take it to a computer shop.

LOCATING THE DATA MAY TAKE A WHILE

Finding the data take a while. Start the search with the DOCUMENTS AND SETTINGS folder of the main USER FOLDER. First search under the primary user folder unless you are certain which user stores the data.

Delete every folder that doesn't contain any information of value. Don't worry about deleting Windows files and folders on the external because they aren't being used.

Windows files being used to operate the computer are on the main or C drive. Only clean up files on the external hard drive, do not delete any Windows or Program files on the C drive.

HARD DRIVE NOT READABLE

In some cases, the old hard drive may be failing or not readable.

We have placed hard drives in a freezer and replaced hard drive motors to get data. On occasion this stuff works and we can retrieve data. If the drive is physically damaged or we cannot retrieve that data, we refer the customer to the hard drive manufacturer. We inform the customer that most drive manufacturers may charge anywhere from $500 to $2000 for a successful data recovery.

Do not consider the case enclosure option as an on-going backup solution when removing data from an old or slow hard drive. Remove the data from the old drive and place the data on a new drive. As stated earlier an older drive has a much greater chance of failing.

SENDING THE HARD DRIVE FOR A DATA RECOVERY

1. DRIVE MANUFACTURER

If sending the drive out for recovery, choose the drive manufacturer. The original hard drive manufacturer should have the best chance to recover data and probably place the most effort into the data save since it was their hard drive that failed.

2. GET A PRICE QUOTE

Receive a price quotation prior to shipping to determine if a successful data recovery is worth the money.

3. SEND INSURED

If sending off the hard drive, don't let the shipping company lose it. Send it insured for the amount paid for a successful data recovery.

DATA RECOVERY PROGRAMS

It may be worth $100-200 for a data recovery program. Recuva and Get Data Back are good data retrieval programs. Look online for free trial programs.

Backup data consistently so a data save recovery won't become necessary in the first place.

28. NOTEBOOK / LAPTOP REPAIRS

There are many negatives to owning a notebook:

- Notebooks are easier to break.
- Notebooks are targeted by thieves and easier to get stolen.
- Out of warranty notebook repairs cost more than desktop repairs.
- Desktops provide better value per dollar spent.
- Notebooks take longer to repair than desktops.
- A notebook screen and keyboard is usually smaller.
- Any liquid such as spilled coffee on a notebook has probably ruined it.
- A dropped notebook when on is probably ruined.
- Fewer computer shops work on notebooks.
- Replacement notebook parts are more expensive and not typically kept in stock.
- Notebooks are more expensive to upgrade.
- Notebook AC chargers are more expensive to replace if they get lost or damaged.
- All that being said, if you absolutely, positively must have the portability or space is that much of an issue, get a notebook."

Despite all these negatives, as a user if you desire portability, then purchase a notebook.

PROTECTING A NOTEBOOK

1. PADDED PROTECTION

Get a padded bag to protect the notebook when transporting. The thicker the padding, the better chance the notebook will survive when the bag is dropped.

2. POWER THE NOTEBOOK OFF WHEN FINISHED

Make sure the notebook power is turned off prior to closing the lid and placing it in the notebook case. A notebook can be in sleep mode and the user doesn't realize it. The notebook then gets placed in the notebook case while still on.

3. DO NOT MOVE THE NOTEBOOK WHEN USING

Our most common notebook hardware repair is replacing hard drives. Above is a photo of a record player. Older people know what a record player is and how to use one.

An older notebook SATA hard drive contains platens. Platens are storage areas for data. Vibrations can knock the platens out of alignment (similar to scratching a record) and ruin the drive. Treat a notebook while powered on similar to a record player playing a record.

The hard drive manufacturers understand this problem and are now manufacturing have developed notebook SSD flash drives, similar to a USB flash drives. Flash drives don't have the moving parts, so are less likely to get damaged due to vibrations.

Turn the notebook completely off before closing the lid and moving. Do not move the notebook when it's on. These tips will keep a notebook working longer.

4. LIQUIDS

Place any drink BEHIND the notebook screen. Placing the drink behind the screen keeps the drink from spilling into the keyboard if it gets knocked over. A liquid spill on a notebook can damage the keyboard and motherboard, leaving someone with either a $400 repair or having to replace a new notebook.

HOW TO HANDLE A LIQUID SPILL ON A LAPTOP:

1. Immediately turn off power. Don't wait to shut down Windows properly.
2. Remove ac adapter from unit and the battery immediately.
3. Keep the screen open and turn the unit upside down to drain liquid off the motherboard.
4. Grab a hair dryer and blow air into keyboard.
5. Leave the notebook upside down for two days to dry out.
6. If possible, place the notebook in rice upside down. Rice absorbs moisture.
7. Let dry for a minimum 3 days and then attempt to turn on.

RESEARCHING NOTEBOOK REPAIRS

Do a search on Google and YouTube for the type of notebook repair to perform and look up repairing the specific model to get instructions. There are plenty of online videos on general notebook repairs for hard drives, memory, keyboards, screens and much more.

NOTEBOOK POWER AC JACK

A common notebook problem is a loose jack connection. The AC power jack is a very small, thin, vulnerable connection part where the AC charger connects to power the notebook and charge the battery.

The jack is placed under stress each time the AC charger is connected and disconnected. Jack damage is caused when a notebook was dropped with the AC charger connected or someone trips over the cord.

On occasion the AC charger can be propped to push up the angle of the connection for a loose jack to work. This is at best a temporary solution; however, if the notebook remains on long enough, at least back up data.

A notebook jack repair is expensive because of the time needed to complete the repair. A notebook jack repair can take up to a day because:

- The first the notebook needs to be disassembled (1-2 hours).
- The jack must either be re-soldered or replaced (up to an hour)
- The notebook must be re-assembled and tested (2 hours). That's a day's worth of work. Expect to pay at least $150 for that type of repair. If a replacement jack has to be special ordered the repair could be delayed up to a week.

If the notebook is less than three years old, consider a jack replacement repair assuming no other damage.

TOUCHSCREEN AND SWIVEL BASED NOTEBOOKS

Touch screen LCDs get damaged and dirty easier because they constantly get touched by dirty fingers. Expect to pay a lot for any out of warranty hardware service.

A notebook digitizer is similar to a smart phone digitizer in that it allows the notebook to be manipulated by touch. Sometimes a digitizer can be broken, but not the notebook screen and vice versa.

On some occasions a notebook screen can be replaced ($50-100) without having to replace a screen and digitizer ($250-400). Determine how important touching the notebook screen instead of using a mouse when deciding whether to pay for a notebook touch screen repair.

CRACKED SCREEN

A cracked screen means that there was trauma to the notebook. Don't order a replacement screen before checking for other damage. Don't order and install a screen, just to later discover that the hard drive was damaged. If the screen is not readable, connect an external monitor to the notebook VGA port to test the notebook.

Assuming the notebook has no other issues, next price out a replacement screen online. Replacement notebook screens can range from $50-$200. Check eBay and Amazon first, then Google the make and model followed by SCREEN.

Check the Return and Replacement Policy prior to ordering parts online.

Make sure that the screen is returnable if it's the incorrect part. We prefer that customers order their own replacement parts. Almost one in four LCD screens shipped to us is the wrong part. We incur the time and cost to return the incorrect part and get the correct replacement and the customer is mad at us, not the company that shipped the incorrect part.

CONDITION A NEW BATTERY

Notebook batteries expire, similar to car batteries. By initially conditioning the battery, it should last longer. The first three times a replacement battery for a notebook is being used, fully charge the battery and run on the battery and run the notebook down until about 10% left on the battery charge. Repower the notebook battery and repeat this process at least two to three times. This procedure will condition the battery and should help make the battery last longer.

UNIVERSAL NOTEBOOK AC CHARGERS

Universal AC notebook chargers are designed to work with different notebooks. Universal chargers are usually packages with multiple size connection tips so the proper connection to the notebook jack can be matched. The universal chargers should auto adjust voltages and amperage output to match that required by the notebook.

Test a replacement universal charger to verify that the AC charger is charging the battery, assuming the battery works. Check to see if the battery is charging by clicking looking at the BATTERY CHARGE LIGHT on the notebook or view the battery icon on the taskbar.

NOTEBOOK POWER MAINENTANCE

Notebooks have sophisticated power management features in Windows. Balance saving power versus better performance. Certain notebooks take a long time to come out of hibernation mode. The unit will perform faster if power management features are turned off.

I turn off power management on my notebook when the unit is plugged into the wall. I set the power settings to blank the screen running on battery within 15 minutes of non-use, but still will turn off sleep mode even on battery.

NOTEBOOK CLEANING

Use compressed air to compress clean any notebook has to be opened for any reason. That saves having to open the notebook just to perform a compress cleaning. If possible, compress clean a notebook once every two to three years.

Dust is drawn inside notebooks just like desktops and notebooks like desktops can overheat and shut down due to dust build-up. Notebooks are much harder to open up and clean. Once the notebook is apart, take a can of compressed air and compress clean the CPU fan and the motherboard.

Purchase a can of compressed air and shoot the air into every open vent. This no-frills cleaning won't remove the built up dust; however, it will recirculate the dust and that may be enough to help an over-heating issue.

Disassemble whatever you are comfortable with in order to shoot compressed air throughout the notebook. Even just moving the dust around inside the notebook is better than doing nothing.

Open notebook repairs are more difficult and expensive. Attempt open notebook repairs only if you have the time and patience.

29. IS FREE STUFF REALLY FREE?

Dictionary definition of the word "free": not costing or charging anything.

EVERYONE WANTS FREE STUFF

"Free" is one of the most searched on words on the Internet. Everyone is looking for a deal and free is good, especially in today's economy. The people that build websites understand that and build their sites to drive web traffic to their sites using the word "free".

TAGS

Websites are built using "tags". A tag is a non-hierarchical keyword of term assigned to a piece of information, such as an image or webpage. Tags are applied to images and pages throughout a website. A tag helps describe an item and allows it to be found again by browsing or searching. The word "free" is very popular with Internet searches and a heavily tagged word.

WEB SEARCH

When a user enters a query into a search engine, the search engine responds with a listing of best-matching web pages according to its criteria, usually with a short summary containing the document's title and sometimes parts of the text. When a user searches on the word "FREE", all images and pages that are tagged with "free" are listed in hierarchical order.

WEBSITE GOALS

A website usually has three distinct goals:

1. Provide Information
2. Generate Leads or draw web traffic
3. Sell Products or provide ad links for visitors to click on

PROVIDE INFORMATION

One goal of a website is to provide information to visitors. Some people will start a website about their hobbies or a public interest issue.

If the site draws enough web traffic, these websites can generate revenue by selling advertising space on the site or through affiliate links. Affiliates are sites that have links to other sites that sell products, and the original site gets a percentage of each sale resulting from following the link.

GENERATE LEADS / DRAW WEB TRAFFIC

One purpose of websites is to collect information. The website will provide something useful or of interest to the site visitor and in exchange the visitor will provide information. Signing up or downloading from most sites usually requires the visitor to provide an email address to receive the free item or service.

An email address is better than a phone number for a telemarketer in terms of the cost to contact the prospect. It costs less money to contact someone using email instead of the phone or a mailing.

Websites place content for the purpose of drawing traffic to the site. These sites place ads on their site and generate revenue when a site visitor clicks on the ads as listed above for the informational websites.

SELL PRODUCTS

Many websites are built to market products. Search engine placement is important for success in order for the website to be found. For the site's products to be found by potential customers, it is important that the website provide tag word content so the search engines can find and list the site.

If your website is supposed to sell tennis balls, post information about tennis balls. Tell the customer about the tennis balls, why they are making a good decision if they purchase your tennis balls, but tell them how to use their tennis balls, where the tennis balls come from, what to do with a tennis ball when you're done with it and other information that the site visitor may find useful. Become an informational resource for your product.

TRACKING COOKIES

Websites place tracking cookies on a site visitor's system to follow their online movements. The tracking cookies transmit that information back to the website for processing. Web whereabouts information is harvested and resold to interested parties. Email, web movements and other information provided at the site are passed on to either an affiliate of that website or other company interested in web demographics.

These tracking cookies can build up on a system. Consider a tracking cookie as a type of roach. One roach in a home may not be much of a problem; however, if that one roach calls his roach buddies to the home, an exterminator may be needed. Tracking cookies will slow down a computer and can cause a computer crash.

THE "FREE" DOWNLOAD

Many "free" sites that get a prospect to their site by promising a free program or file download. In exchange for a free download, a website is probably placing tracking cookies on a computer.

FREE STUFF GETS HIDDEN

Free program download sites usually strategically place multiple program downloads at a prime position on their site hoping that a user may mistakenly download the wrong program.

Each time that incorrect program is downloaded, that program's owner pays the website money for the download referral. The website makes money per each download; it doesn't matter the consumer downloaded the incorrect program, that site still makes money. It's in the site's interest to trick the user into downloading the wrong program.

The free program or file download can be hidden within pages, forcing a user to review ads and other download alternatives before finding the actual program the user sought. A user must provide contact information to get the "free" stuff. Minimally a valid email address must be provided and additional information may be required such as sex, age and zip code.

JUNK EMAILS

By providing an email address, the user is open to receiving junk email from affiliates of the website that either pay or agree to share information. The website collecting the email probably shares that along with any other information provided. A user can receive over 100 emails a day soliciting for different products and services.

Nothing on the Internet is free. Personal information is being exchanged for the freebie being downloaded.

AVOID THE CRAP

Most free download sites automatically select other programs for a system to download. Uncheck any unwanted file downloads to a system. NEVER USE EXPRESS DOWNLOAD. Express Downloads will download other programs besides the desired program. Select the CUSTOM option and uncheck all the other programs the site has checked to download onto the system.

USE A SECOND EMAIL ADDRESS

To avoid junk emails, setup a secondary email address. Free email accounts can be acquired at Hotmail, Gmail or Yahoo. Use a secondary email address to prevent the primary email address from getting compromised. Check messages in the secondary email account once a week to check that you don't miss anything of importance.

SURF ANONYMOUS PROGRAMS

Programs like PROXIFY, VPN and SURF ANONYMOUS permit a web surfer to surf the Internet anonymously. Prior to surfing, login to Proxify or other surf anonymously website. From that site enter the address of the site to visit anonymously. A computer IP address gets "bounced" or moved from server to server, making it difficult for the website to get a trace on it.

Internet stealth surfing programs are now available so the Internet can be surfed without the user being tracked.

ASK THIS QUESTION BEFORE DOWNLOADING "FREE" STUFF

Is the file, program or information being downloaded worth the giving up of your personal information and the possible future solicitations?

Don't get sucked into the "FREE" syndrome. Use a secondary email address for downloading "free" programs or signing up for "free" specials or newsletters.

30. WIRELESS REPAIRS

ISP stands for **I**nternet **S**ervice **P**rovider. An ISP provides a gateway through phone lines, cable, and cellular or wireless by which an electronic device can gain access to the Internet. We used the word electronic device instead of computer since many people use iPads, PDAs and smart phones to get online. We review four types of Internet Providers: dial up, DSL, cable or FIOS and wireless.

FIOS / CABLE

The fastest computer and devices Internet service for home and small business is provided by cable and high speed phone optical companies. Home services begin between $30-40 per month for Internet. Both the cable and phone companies attempt to bundle Internet access along with phone and television at a higher cost.

The higher speed ISP service is better for watching online videos and television. The local living area may determine the service based on availability. People in a rural or developing area may not have access to the higher speed services or only get a choice of one high speed carrier.

WIRELESS

Providers like Clear, Cricket, T-Moblie, Verizon and Sprint provide wireless Internet access. Speed of service typically ranges from 3G to 5G. The higher the G number, the faster the wireless.

Wireless Internet is an alternative to people just want wireless Internet access without extra television channels and services. Companies like Clear and Cricket provide users with a portable USB wireless device that attaches to a notebook.

The wireless USB device generates its own signal that permits access the Internet anywhere their service can pick up a signal tower. Monthly plans for this type of service begin between $30-40 per month.

SMART PHONES

Smart phone providers provide data plans for Internet access and data exchange through the smart phone providers service. Smart phones are becoming increasingly popular for people to access Facebook, YouTube and send text messages.

SATELLITE

Satellite provides offer Internet access; however, the service is brokered out through third party companies. DISH was purchased by ATT, another wireless provider. I personally always preferred a hard wired cable connection to satellite.

INTERNET HOTSPOTS

A hotspot is an unsecured wireless network that anyone with a wireless capable device can gain Internet access. A hotspot could be located at an Internet café, coffee shop or any other public location.

Do not log onto any secure accounts while using a hotspot, especially if using someone else's or a shared computer. The computer could have a key logger program that is capturing and recording passwords for a hacker to use.

SKYPE

Skype is a service owned by Microsoft that permits users to make voice and video calls and chats over the Internet. Calls to other users within the Skype service are free, while calls to both traditional landline telephones and mobile phones can be made for a fee using a debit-based user account system.

Skype has become popular for its additional features which include instant messaging, file transfer, and video conferencing. Look into Skype if you have friends or relatives overseas.

WIRELESS

Wireless telecommunications is the transfer of information between two points that are physically not connected. Distances can be short, as a few meters as in television remote control; or long ranging from thousands to millions of kilometers for deep-space radio communications.

Wireless can be used by various devices such as mobile and portable two-way radios, cellular telephones, personal digital assistants (PDAs), I pads and wireless networking.

WIRELESS NETWORK

A wireless network refers to any type of computer network that is not connected by cables. It is a method by which homes and businesses avoid the costly process of running cables into a home or building.

Many homes and businesses have wireless setups which include computers, tablets, smart televisions, security systems, phones and printers. The biggest advantage of a wireless network is that it is more convenient than running cables between computers and printers.

DISADVANTAGES

Potential disadvantages of going wireless are speed and security. For example one may get better performance watching a movie on the Internet using a physical connection versus watching wireless. Make sure that your wireless network is password protected to prevent unauthorized use.

INCREASE SIGNAL STRENGTH

The signal emitted from a wireless network may not be as strong in different areas. Place the wireless router in an open area as to not to restrict the signal. Place the antenna vertically. If the signal isn't strong, move the router to a different location or purchase a signal booster. Sometimes changing the Channel signal may help because other services locally may be using the same channel. Secure the signal, so others cannot access the signal.

PRINTERS

Wireless printers are used when cabling a printer or location is an issue or multiple people need printer access. Basic network problems such as a re-assigned IP address can cause a printer not to print.

One option is to keep a USB printer cable handy so the printer can be physically connected to a computer for printing if the wireless doesn't work properly.

KEYBOARDS AND MICE

Wireless keyboards are convenient to watch a movie or work on a large screen TV or LCD that requires distance from the user. A user doesn't have to walk across the room to pause the movie. Wireless keyboards are convenient when giving a power point presentation in front of an audience.

Wireless mice are convenient to use on an airplane or when space is limited. They are also useful when watching a movie on a computer. One doesn't have to get up and walk across the room to pause the movie.

WEBCAM

Wireless webcams are used mostly for security reasons and remote access. A webcam can be setup to observe either the home or workplace from a remote location over the Internet. Many notebooks and tablets have built in webcams for video use.

WIRELESS CONTINUES TO CONNECT AND DISCONNECT

If all devices on the network have the same problem with the Internet it is likely an issue with the cable or modem. If only one computer is disconnecting and reconnecting, it's likely a problem with the computer.

PHONE NOT CONNECTING TO WIFI

Reset the Network Settings. Select SETTINGS, and ensure that, AIRPLANE MODE is off. Then open GENERAL or SETTINGS and select RESET NETWORK SETTINGS.

WIRELESS REPAIRS

If the wireless connection to a device is not working:

1. MOVE AND TEST THE DEVICE TO A DIFFERENT WIRELESS HOTSPOT.

   Use the Principle of Halves to determine if the problem is with the device or the wireless network.

2. RESET THE DEVICE

   Right Click on the WIRELESS ICON on the bottom right of the taskbar and Select / RESET the wireless on the device.

3. PHYICALLY TURN OFF AND RESTART THE DEVICE.

4. PHYICALLY PULL THE POWER PLUG FROM THE ROUTER, COUNT TO 10 AND RESTART THE DEVICE.

Wireless is convenient and the way of the world. A hard-wired connection if available is better for security and speed.

31. WEB BROWSER & EMAIL REPAIRS

Web Surfing is similar to having the ultimate TV remote control at your fingertips except that instead of having 25-1000 stations to choose from, there are somewhere in the gazillion for web page choices. The number is so high in fact that they are running out of IP addresses and will have to expand the number pool. That's a lot of web pages.

WEB BROSWER

The web browser is used to surf the Internet. Microsoft Edge and Microsoft Explorer are the most widely used browser and the only browser that permits a computer to get Windows updates. Other popular browsers are Firefox and Chrome and Safari by Apple.

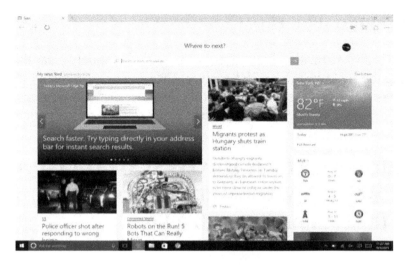

Viewing a web page on the World Wide Web begins by typing the URL of the page into a web browser or clicking on or following a hyperlink to a page. The web browser then initiates a series of communication messages to display the page.

WHAT HAPPENS WHEN A WEB ADDRESS IS ENTERED IN A BROWSER

- Enter the web address of the website to visit.
- The web address is assigned a specific DNS number, in this case 173.201.144.1.
- The browser then requests the page request across the Internet to the computer at that particular address.
- The request goes to a particular application port in the underlying Internet Protocol Suite so that the computer receiving the request can distinguish an HTTP request from other network protocols it may be servicing such as e-mail delivery; the HTTP protocol normally uses port 80.
- Once the request is received and processed, the web page appears.

ADDING FAVORITES

Websites to revisit on a consistent basis can be added under FAVORITES to make it quicker and easier to get to the site. Any site listed under the FAVORITES can be accessed by selecting it.

- Click the ADD TO FAVORITES bar Icon on the top left of the toolbar.
- Choose the ADD to FAVORITES from the drop-down menu and click the ADD button.

CLEARING JUNK FROM A BROWSER

Web browsers pick up junk when on the web. Routinely clear the browser settings by using the BROWSER RESET feature. Clearing or resetting a browser is a good way to fix basic web browser problems. If the browser displays pop-ups or doesn't work, reset the browser. Consider resetting the browser settings at least once a week.

Learn to CLEAR BROWSING DATA AND RESET the web browser. Also have a second browser installed on the computer as a backup.

TO RESET THE BROWSER SETTINGS

- Select THE MULTIPLE DOTS ON THE TOP RIGHT OF THE BROWER
- Open the menu and search for CLEAR BROWSER or RESET BROWSER. This option may be found under ADVANCED SETTINGS.

MULTIPLE BROWSERS

Every Windows based computer has either Microsoft Edge or Internet Explorer. Download and keep either Google Chrome or Mozilla Firefox on the computer as a second browser for backup purposes, in case the primary browser stops working.

Assume that someone is tracking your online movements.

That website you just visited may have placed a tracking cookie on a system. It could be spyware. It could be the government. Everyone wants to collect information. To surf anonymously, Google "Surf anonymously". Sites like Proxify offer anonymous web surfing and downloading.

EMAIL

An email is an electronic letter sent over the Internet. Most people use a computer to send and receive emails because it's more convenient and travels faster than writing a letter.

An email message consists of three or four components, the envelope, the header, and the body and possible attachment. The header contains control information, including the sender email and one or more recipient addresses. Normally descriptive information is added, such as a subject header field and a message submission date/time stamp

VIRUS CARRIERS

Emails and email attachments are the most common means to get a virus on a computer. Someone sends an email with an attachment. The attachment is opened and immediately the computer begins to act strange. That attachment contained a virus that has attached itself to the computer once it was opened.

In some cases, the virus wasn't sent intentionally. The sender didn't know they attached an infected file and didn't mean it; however, the computer is infected just the same.

EMAIL PRECAUTIONS

Take the following precautions when sending or receiving email:

1. DON'T CLICK ON ANY .EXE FILE

Any executable file is any file that has an EXE suffix and starts a program. Any type attachment has the potential to be infected. Some ISP servers don't allow the downloading of EXE files because of the infection potential. Don't click to open any executable file, unless the EXE file is expected.

2. OPEN EMAIL ON THE ISP's SERVER

Log onto the ISP's server to open, edit and send email and email attachments. EXAMPLE: If Comcast is your ISP, login to Comcast's website with your email address and password. Once in, open and check email and attachments. Any viruses being opened are on the ISP's server, not the system's hard drive. The computer being used has less chance of being infected.

It is safer to open email attachments on the ISP's server than to download emails and open attachments directly to a computer using Microsoft Outlook.

Downloading and opening mail on a computer increases the probability of infecting the computer by 30-40%. Why take the risk?

WEBMAIL

Webmail is using the Internet Service Provider's server and email account to open, send and receive emails. Webmail is safer instead of downloading emails from the ISP directly to the computer then opening them in Outlook Express or Outlook.

Companies like Google, Yahoo and Microsoft provide free webmail services like Gmail, Hotmail or Yahoo. The user logs to the ISP website. At the ISP site, the user then logs into their webmail account using their email address and password. Once logged in, the user can send and receive email, open attachments, forward messages while all being done at the ISP's website.

Webmail is much safer than downloading emails to the computer and opening them using Microsoft Outlook Express or Outlook. The computer is not exposed to any potential viruses and junk emails can be managed much better. Ask the Internet Service Provider if they have a Webmail option.

3. GET BROWSER UPDATES.

Keep the web browser updated with the latest security patches. Windows in most cases will automatically update, but it's a good idea to manually check for updates at least once a month.

SPAMMING

Spam email is unsolicited email sent with the purpose of eliciting a response from a recipient. The email may ask for someone to spend money or provide personal information. Most spam carries an advertising message. It's not legal and most ISPs don't permit it; however, that doesn't stop the spammers. The spammer will then either use or sell the responder's information to marketers or whoever wants to pay for the information.

HOW TO LIMIT SPAM

CONTACT THE ISP

The ISP is the first line of defense against spam emails. The ISP can help adjust your mail settings so that spam email gets blocked; however, be careful. The ISP can sometimes identify good mail as spam and accidently delete it or place it in a BLOCKED or SPAM folder.

This is called a "false positive" event. One major Internet provider rejects up to 12 million e-mails a day because the addresses don't match the real user's email addresses – a sure sign of a spammer. Occasionally check other email folders besides the INBOX in case some important emails were accidently placed in the SPAM box by mistake.

WHITE LISTING

Many ISPs offer "white listing" options for their users. White listing means the email recipient can add the email addresses of the senders from who they want mail to a list on their mail account. Messages sent from anyone who is NOT on the "white list" are automatically placed on a "black list" and refused by the ISP.

OPT IN EMAIL

Opt in e-mail is a term used when someone is given the option to receive "bulk" e-mail, that is, e-mail that is sent to many people at the same time. Obtaining opt in permission before sending e-mail is critical because without it, the e-mail is unsolicited bulk email, better known as spam.

Unconfirmed opt-in

A new subscriber first gives his or her address to the list software, but no steps are taken to verify that this address actually belongs to the person. This can cause e-mail from the mailing list to be considered spam.

Confirmed opt-in

A new subscriber asks to be subscribed to the mailing list, but unlike unconfirmed opt-in, a confirmation e-mail is sent to verify it was really them. Many believe the person must not be added to the mailing list unless an explicit step is taken, such as clicking a special web link or sending back a reply e-mail. This ensures that no person can subscribe someone else out of malice or error.

UNSUBSCRIBE

In theory a user can click the "unsubscribe" link from email solicitations and be removed from the list. Be advised that it may take a couple of weeks for the party to comply. Sometimes the request can be ignored.

DON'T REPLY TO SPAM

Don't reply to spam. Don't respond to anything not requested. Once a response is sent, the other side has captured the email address and will really become a nuisance.

USE MULTIPLE EMAIL ADDRESSES

Use a "throw away email account for any online "free stuff" or offers.

BE SKEPTICAL

Beware of email offers that sound too good to be true. No one from Nigeria wants to give you $1,000,000 for brokering a deal and that beautiful Russian girl has no interest in meeting you. Spammers use "phishing" schemes to dupe people and get credit card or social security numbers. Don't respond to these ads.

MOST COMMON EMAIL PROBLEMS

1. CAN SEND BUT NOT RECEIVE or CAN RECEIVE BUT NOT SEND

- Check the spelling of the email to send.
- Check the MAIL SERVER setup information in the email program. If problem is SENDING, check the OUTGOING info.
- If information looks correct, retype in the same information and attempt to resend again.
- Check for viruses and spyware.

2. CANNOT SEND OUT A PARTICULAR FILE

The file or attachment to the file may be too large. Most mail servers limit files to 10MB. Either break up the file and send the file in smaller pieces or find a site that will allow a larger email file attachment to be sent.

3. TIME OUT ERRORS WHEN SENDING EMAIL

- There's a problem with the Anti-Virus or Firewall. As a test, turn them off and send the email again. If the email now transmits, the protection software is causing the problem.
- There's a problem with the email server or the email account.
- Check the mail server information. If it looks correct, delete the account and reset the same information. Send the same email from a different account or computer.

4. CANNOT RECEIVE EMAILS FROM PEOPLE

- Make sure that their email address is not blacklisted by your ISP.
- Make sure that they have your correct email address.
- Check that any email spam filter isn't set too high. Check the SPAM filer to find out if emails are getting placed there.
- Scan for viruses and spyware.

5. EMAILS GOING TO OUTBOX BUT NOT SENDING

- Communication problem between Outlook and the outgoing mail server, so the email is stuck in Outbox because Outlook can't connect to the mail server to send it. .
- Check with the email address provider and make sure the mail server settings are up to date.

ALWAYS ASSUME SOMEONE OTHER THAN YOUR INTENDED RECEPIENT IS READING YOUR EMAIL

When you send email always assume that your mail will be read by someone other than the intended party. This may help filter your content when writing something especially writing when angry.

Use email wisely and have multiple email accounts.

32. DOWNLOADING PROBLEMS

DOWNLOAD AND UPLOAD

When a file is downloaded, it's transferred from a computer somewhere on the Internet to your computer. The most commonly downloaded files are programs, updates, or other kinds of files such as game demos, music and video files, or documents. Downloading can mean copying information from any source to a computer or other device, such as copying favorite songs to a portable music player.

Downloading is now the preferred method for distribution of software. It's less expensive and more efficient for a company to setup a download site then to mass produce, label and distribute software on DVDs through retail stores. For buyers, it's easier to download a program online. Downloads on viral and programs updates are commonplace.

DOWNLOADING BASICS

1. KNOW WHAT YOU'RE DOWNLOADING

First find the correct program or file to download. Check that the computer downloading to has the required system specifications and operating system needed to run the file or program.

2. KNOW WHERE THE DOWNLOAD IS GOING

Downloads are normally placed in a folder titled DOWNLOADS. Sometimes it's more convenient to direct a download to the DESKTOP, in order to access it immediately without having to check the DOWNLOADS folder. Be advised that sending everything to the DESKTOP can make for a cluttered desktop for viewing.

3. SAVE IMMEDIATELY

Once the download completes, copy the download to a DVD or USB flash or hard drive off the computer. Do this prior to opening or executing the downloaded file, so it's safely off the computer. Once the program is executed, it's harder to backup.

Remember to back up to a separate location off the computer. Copy the download to an external USB flash or hard drive prior to installing the program. It's easier to re-install the download from a separate source than to re-download the program from the site if the program downloaded was a paid program. Proof of purchase may be required to re-download the file.

DOWNLOAD PROBLEM TROUBLESHOOTING

If the download doesn't start or complete follow these steps to get the problem corrected.

1. CHECK THE SPECIFICATIONS AND READ THE ERROR MESSAGE

The message may explain why the download failed. Attempt to follow any given message instructions. Sometimes a download may not begin because the system downloading to doesn't have the minimum requirements for the software. The system operating system may be dated; the system may not have enough memory or drive space. Check the program requirements and match them to the system downloading to.

2. **UNINSTALL PREVIOUS VERSIONS OF THE SOFTWARE**

   First uninstall any older version of the program under PROGRAMS or ADD / REMOVE PROGRAMS, to prevent a program conflict on the download.

3. **CLOSE ALL APPLICATIONS**

   Close any open programs. Sometimes an open program may cause a problem with a download.

4. **UNINSTALL ANY COMPETITIORS**

   Uninstall any similar type software from the system. EXAMPLE: If an anti-virus program, it may ask to un-install any competitors on the system. Remove the anti-virus program the download is replacing.

5. **UPDATE AND CLEAR THE BROWSER**

   Check that the browser has current updates. Sometimes a browser security update may need to be updated to get the download. Reset the browser settings and try again.

6. **CHECK FOR VIRUSES, and MALWARE**

   A virus or malware file could be causing problems with the download.

ILLEGAL DOWNLOADS

It's against the law to download copyrighted without paying for it, PERIOD. Remember that someone spent a lot of money to produce that song or movie and are entitled to get paid for their work.

Just remember that there's no difference between illegally downloading and reaching over the counter and taking money out of a cash drawer in a store. If you're the type to illegally copy DVDs, you're probably already illegally downloading and this warning is not going to convince you otherwise.

Be careful and know what you are downloading.

33. DUMB COMPUTER STUFF

Listed are stupid things that either I've done or have seen employees or customers do with a computer. DON'T DO THEM!

1. UPGRADING TOO SOON

I wanted to be the first in the neighborhood to have Windows XP when it was first released. I wasn't one of those people that had to wait outside the CompUSA store at midnight; however, I did purchase and install it on my system within 24 hours of release.

It took six months before I was finally rid of all the blue screen problems and lockups and that only happened after a service pack upgrade. I lost some old programs that ran under Windows 95 because they wouldn't work on XP.

Fight that impulse to be the first on the block to put that brand new operating system on your system or purchase that brand new computer with the new fastest chip on the block. Don't be first. The first release of any new software product has some issues. Most of those issues get corrected in the first Service Pack release.

WAIT AT LEAST 6 MONTHS from initial program release to upgrade any operating system or any hardware upgrade.

If programmers and quality control personnel decided when to release software for distribution one of following two things would happen:

- Software would never get released because the programmers would want it perfect.
- The released products would work much better and users would be happier.

The management and marketing people assign the software release dates and the programmers do their best to meet their deadlines. Why rush to install and run a just released product or program? It can be painful being first. Most software companies release a Service Pack release within 3-6 months of the product introduction that corrects most of the problems that users had to deal with in the initial release.

Wait to purchase a new computer, smart phone or other product that has the latest, fastest, state of the art processor or features. The price should drop on computers within 90 days. Buying just released hardware in most cases is like purchasing a stock right after it's offered to the general public. It's at its highest selling point. Wait awhile and get the same performance for less money.

2. BEING CARELESS WITH A NOTEBOOK

One time I accidently spilled a drink on my notebook and ruined it. Another time I tripped over my notebook AC charger cable while it was connected to the wall. My clumsiness caused a problem with the jack and the jack had to be soldered. Normal cost for that repair is $150. I received the store owner discount. Be careful using a notebook on a bed without a cooler underneath to dissipate the heat buildup.

Walking around with a turned on notebook, working in an area where someone can trip over the AC power cord cable and placing a drink down next to the notebook are other reasons a notebook can get damaged.

3. OPEN AN EMAIL ATTACHMENT DIRECTLY ON THE COMPUTER WITHOUT FIRST SCANNING FOR VIRUSES

There is absolutely no reason not to open email attachments on the ISPs server. Log onto the ISP's site to open email and email attachments. Do not download and open emails using Outlook Express or Outlook. The odds that a computer will get infected by opening an email or email attachment directly on the computer increase by 40%.

4. GIVE OUT BANK OR OTHER PASSWORD BASED ON AN EMAIL REQUEST

A phishing email is an email that looks innocent enough – bank XYZ is updating their records and wants to verify the account logon and password. It's "fishing" for someone to give up their online password so they can log into the account and steal your money.

NEVER respond to any email asking for a password update. Any email requests of this type should be verified by emailing the company from the company's website or calling the company for verification.

5. MOVING A NOTEBOOK WHILE ON

Constantly moving a notebook while on is bad for the hard drive. I occasionally do it even though I know it's not good for the notebook hard drive. Limit movement of the notebook while on, including opening and closing of the lid.

6. USING A NOTEBOOK WITH A FRAYED CHARGER

Using a notebook with a charger that has a damaged charger or open wires is a recipe for disaster. A notebook charger with a frayed AC cord is a fire hazard and causes the notebook to overheat. A bad charger may output incorrect voltage or amperage, which can cause damage to the notebook, battery or both.

7. IMPROPERLY SHUT DOWN THE COMPUTER

Sometimes we get lazy or are in a hurry, so we press the power button to shut down the computer instead of using the proper Windows shut down process. Constantly turning off a computer this way WILL corrupt Windows and cause problems in the future.

8. NOT SECURING WIRELESS

Not pass wording a wireless network is an open invitation for hackers. Assume that someone will use an open wireless signal and possibly attempt to hack into the system.

Evil doers could use an open account to send spam email or worse, do illegal stuff and the FBI will knock on your door. Your system will slow down online if someone is "piggybacking" or using your wireless signal for their personal Internet access.

9. LEND OUT A NOTEBOOK

Lending out a notebook to someone is a sure way to get the system returned with a virus or spyware, damage or pornographic popups that may cause embarrassment if the significant other borrows the same notebook and up pops some porn.

10. USE A CHEAP SURGE PROTECTOR

We get many systems with blown power supplies because people don't spend $20-30 to get a decent surge protector. A $7.99 surge protector is using an extension cord only. Spend $20-30 and get a surge protector that has at least 1200 joules and some type of equipment damage warranty.

11. DOWNLOADING PORN OR OTHER "FREE" SOFTWARE FROM A TORRENT WEBSITE

A torrent website is a site that posts movies and programs for illegal downloading. Besides being illegal, torrents are good places to acquire viruses, spyware and malware on the computer.

Follow these tips to keep out of trouble.

34. ONLINE SAFETY

Everyone is concerned about online safety, including the online crooks. The crooks are concerned because if people wise up, they may have to quit online thievery and look for a real job.

TYPES OF ONLINE ISSUES

- Annoyance
- Privacy / Invasion
- Theft or Identity Theft
- Personal Safety

ANNOYANCE

An annoyance is an unwanted online solicitation. An annoyance usually takes the form of junk email promoting some offer that wasn't requested and there is no interest. It takes about the same amount of time to press the delete a junk email as it does to throw out the junk email in the trash. Annoyance issues while a nuisance, aren't really safety related and can be controlled to some extent.

PRIVACY / INVASION

Privacy invasion issues can be distressing and difficult to address. An example of an invasion of privacy is when someone slanders or posts a photo, video or information about another person online. Removing unwanted content from the Internet can be a problem and the laws haven't caught up to this type of problem.

THEFT / INDENTITY THEFT

Identity theft problems are very serious. A person gets tricked into giving up their personal information and as a result gets accounts compromised and credit damaged. A person could spend days, weeks or years repairing damaged credit.

PERSONAL SAFETY

Personal safety is the most serious problem. Chat rooms and social networking sites are the most popular and widely used methods to meet and interact with people. Anyone can fabricate any story anything about themselves.

CYBERBULLYING

Cyber bullying is bullying that takes place over digital devices like smart phones, computers, and tablets. Cyber bullying includes sending or posting, negative, harmful, or false content about someone else. Cyber bullying can include sharing personal or private information about someone else causing embarrassment or humiliation. The most common places where cyber bullying occurs are:

- Social Media, such as Facebook, Instagram, Snapchat, and Twitter
- Phone text messaging or email
- Instant Message (via devices, email provider services, apps, and social media messaging features)

Cyber bullying can harm the online reputation of the person being bullied and the person or persons doing the bullying will not looked with a favorable light.

Digital devices offer an ability to immediately and continuously communicate 24 hours a day, so it can be difficult for children experiencing cyber bullying to find relief.

LAWS

All states have criminal laws that apply to bullying but not all have special statutes that apply to cyber bulling or bullying that takes place outside of school. If aware of someone being cyber bullied, make a call to the local police department to get direction on how to proceed.

ONLINE PREDATORS

An entire book could be written regarding protecting children from online predators. Dateline produced a whole series on Internet predators. It gives insight into what type of loser that potentially can setup a meeting with a child on the Internet if parents aren't careful. Children are disposed to give out personal information. The following suggestions may help keep children safe on the Internet:

ONLINE CHILD SAFETY TIPS

SET THE GROUNDRULES

Set a list of conditions for children prior to them using the computer. Place limits on:

- **Priors** – does homework need to be completed prior to online access?
- **Time** – how long can they have access?
- **Supervision** - Do they need to be supervised when online?
- **Passwords** - Will the unit be pass- worded? Who will have password access?
- **Site restriction** – Restrict questionable sites.
- **Penalties** – Appropriate punishment if rules are broken.

CHAT ROOMS

A chat room is where computer users meet online and have a "conversation" with others. Monitor children if they have access chat rooms. Sit down with them and discuss what is appropriate and not appropriate. Setup an account in an appropriate chat room on a topic that they have interest and show them how to chat online appropriately. Teach them how to answer and what not to tell people online.

CHECK WEB HISTORY AND EMAIL ADDRESSES

Check the browser history, to see where your child has been. If their browsing history folder is empty it is being cleared and you may need to purchase a stealth program.

STEALTH PROGRAM

A stealth program will follow a user's movements on the Internet, record their keystrokes and send a report without their knowledge. As a parent I believe it's better to know the worse than to assume the best. Some popular stealth programs include KGB and Net Nanny. Windows has some spying tools worth investigating.

CHECK EMAIL

Check their INBOX and SENT folders. See if there's anything unusual. Check in DELETED messages. Deleted messages remain in that folder unless the Deleted folder is cleaned out as well. If the DELETED folder is empty, again an indication that there may have a problem. The RECYCLE BIN will hold deleted items for 30 days unless someone thought to also remove all items from the RECYCLE BIN separately.

STOP IN UNANNOUNCED

Stop in your child's room unannounced on occasion. If they immediately close the browser, check their web history later.

DO NOT GIVE OUT INFORMATION

Make sure children NEVER give out personal information on-line – last name, address, age, phone number, passwords, social security number, or email any pictures.

KEEP COMMUNICATION OPEN

Make all children aware to inform you if they receive any message that makes them feel uncomfortable.

NO MEETINGS

The Internet is a place where sickos and perverts hunt for young children. Explain to children what can happen if they arrange a meeting with an Internet acquaintance. I went into graphic detail with my daughter about what could happen and she's watched enough Law and Order SVU to understand what can happen if she makes a bad decision.

GOOGLE YOUR CHILD'S NAME

Perform an online check of your child to see if there is anything posted. Google your child's name and check the results. If there is something posted that you don't want online, contact the website. If they resist removing it, contact the local law enforcement agency to get information on how to get the information removed.

CHILD WEBSITES

There are many good websites designed for children. Your child's school should have a list of approved websites. Teach children about online kids search engines. We listed a couple in our FREE STUFF section.

SMART PHONES

Smart phones can be difficult to monitor. Attempt to apply the same computer monitoring techniques to smart phones: You may opt to take the "bad parent" approach and demand the phone for your review. Check with the wireless provider and smartphone provider for an app that can monitor the phone user's activity. Google "SMART PHONE MONITORING APPS" and see what's available. Always check the free apps first.

TEXTING

We need to spend a minute to discuss texting. There are some people I must text to get a response. As an older person, I hate to text. I don't see the sense having to spend an extra two minutes to type out something on a mini keyboard two small for my fingers when I can just pick up the phone, press one digit and speak to someone or at least leave a message. I was discussing the negatives of texting and one of my techs explained texting to me:

"Texting is when you want to communicate with someone, but not speak to them".

When I asked him about voicemail, his response was that one always runs the risk that the person will pick up the phone. Texting is popular for students when in class or somewhere where a smart phone ringing is inappropriate. So now I text, but only when I absolutely have to.

SOCIAL NETWORKING

Social Networking on the Internet is the preferred method to interact and meet people. Facebook, Twitter, YouTube, Pinterest, Instagram, dating sites, blogs, and chat rooms, the Internet is one gigantic coffee house with millions of people conversing 24-7. Social network sites are the best hunting ground for crooks to run scams and for users to possibly get malware or spyware on their computer. The following suggestions may help when online:

- Use UPDATED antivirus, spyware removal and malware software.
- Open all emails and email attachments ON YOUR ISPs SERVER. Do not download emails and open in Microsoft Outlook Express or Outlook.
- Do not open any email attachments without first scanning for a virus.
- Open any suspect emails or attachments, attempt to open them on a secondary computer, not the main computer.
- Get a 2nd free email address from Gmail, yahoo or Hotmail and give use that email address out to all online offers or any free downloads.
- Never give a real email address or other personal information when chatting online.
- Use anti spamming filtering.
- Password a wirelesses network.
- Use a combination of letters and numbers for online passwords.
- Do not to keep personal information like social security number or credit card numbers on the computer.
- Never send personal information online unless first confirming the request.
- Never give any online vendor access to any checking account. Pay by credit card, not debit card.
- Sign up for a PayPal account use PayPal whenever possible. Setup a separate checking account for PayPal and other online purchases. Keep the bare minimum and fund only as necessary.

ONLINE SAFETY TIPS

1. USE A SECURE WIRELESS

Every home wireless network should be password-protected. Other users will slow down the network and the network could be used for more sinister motives. The easiest technique to protect wireless is to encrypt the wireless network so a password must be entered to access the network.

2. AVOID PUBLIC COMPUTERS AND WIFI

Using a public computer can leave personal information exposed. Public computers can be infected with spyware, malware and key loggers designed to track movements online and harvest (steal) your passwords.

3. KEEP SOFTWARE UP TO DATE

This means ALL software, not just Windows. Cyber crooks look for vulnerabilities in any software. Don't run an anti-virus program a couple of years old even if it is still providing up to date protection. Upgrade to the most recent version. The programming built into the software is always being improved.

4. USE HTTPS SITES FOR BUYING

Check the website and check that HTTPS is at the beginning of the address. HTTPS stands for Hypertext Transfer Protocol Secure. HTTPS encrypts the connection between the PC and the website being visited. Though HTTPS isn't 100% secure, it can help prevent other parties from hacking into the network and gaining access to information.

5. INSTALL A LINK-CHECKER PLUG IN

A link checker will show a badge next the web link and indicate whether the site is safe or not. Download and install WOT - Web of Trust.

6. **PHYSICAL SECURITY**

Don't neglect your notebook especially if it's being used in a public place. A thief can snatch it and walk away in a couple of seconds. A thief that has a notebook has access to personal information.

A notebook lock may not keep a thief from cutting the cable but may deter a potential criminal. Lock a screen from viewing before leaving a notebook unattended even for a short period of time.

7. **USE GOOD PASSWORDS**

Use a combination of words, numbers and symbols. Refer to the Passwords section.

8. **CHECK YOUR CREDIT REPORT EACH YEAR**

Check your credit report each year to make sure that a new account hasn't been opened in your name. Any U.S. citizen is entitled to a free credit report from one of the three major credit agencies – Equifax, Experian or TransUnion through annualcreditreport.com.

9. **USE A VIRTUAL CREDIT CARD**

Ask your bank or Credit Card Company if they can provide a virtual credit card number for online purchases. A virtual credit card number is good for one use only. The seller will only have name and ship to address and phone; however, no other information, so your credit card information is secure.

10. **PASSWORD PROTECT AND LOCK DOWN A PHONE**

Make sure to have a password on your phone, so if it is lost or stolen, it cannot be accessed. Make sure the GPS tracker is activated, so the phone location can be traced if necessary.

Phones can get viruses. Lock down any phone and download a phone antivirus application. Download The Lookout Mobile Security App at PC World for an Android-based phone.

Practice online safety and secure wireless.

35. ADDITIONAL HELP SOURCES

Even a knowledgeable tech can get stuck sometimes. Listed below are some help options that may assist in a computer crisis:

1. CHECK WITH THE COMPANY THAT IS RESPONSIBLE FOR THE PROBLEM

That doesn't necessarily mean to call the computer company. If the problem is with an accounting package that doesn't work properly after an upgrade, contact the accounting software company. If the printer makes a clacking noise and the print carriage doesn't move, contact the printer company or better yet go out and purchase a new printer. If the computer crashes after a device driver update, check with the device driver manufacturer.

2. RESEARCH THE PROBLEM ONLINE

Enter the error message or problem in GOOGLE or other search engine. Most likely another user has experienced the problem and placed the solution online.

3. CHECK THE MANUAL AND HELP ME FILES

The problem may be described in the manual or in a READ ME FILE on the computer.

4. CHECK WITH YOUR GURU

A computer guru knows more about computers than you. It could be a family member, relative, or the IT guy at work or the geek at the computer store.

5. CALL THE COMPUTER MANUFACTURER OR CHECK THEIR SITE

There may be a known problem between a specific manufacturer computer and a particular hardware of software problem. Check their website FAQs. If the problem is hardware, it may be repaired free if it's anything related to the computer hardware and the computer is still under warranty.

6. TAKE THE COMPUTER TO A COMPUTER REPAIR SHOP

A computer service center is the last resort because it will cost money. Prior to the check-in, ask them if they have any experience with the type of problem being experienced.

WINDOWS ONLINE HELP SYSTEM

The Windows Help option can be accessed from the menu by selecting HELP from the menu. Select the specific help topic. Windows will inquire about accessing online help, which is more extensive

WINDOWS TROUBLESHOOTER

Select Windows Troubleshooter under help to get additional help with a problem The Troubleshooter will take you through a series of steps to help you narrow the cause of the problem. To access the Troubleshooter, Select PC SETTINGS and TROUBLESHOOT.

CONTACTING HELP

PHONE

Only use phone if the phone call and support time is free. It's frustrating enough to deal with a phone support tree, but really frustrating if having to pay for substandard to mediocre help as well.

ON-LINE CHAT

Online chat is texting on-line with a technical support person. This option is offered by many company websites. Select the Chat or Online Chat option, follow the instructions and wait for a tech to type. Introduce yourself and answer the question as prompted.

I really like the online chat support option. The online chat technical help is usually manned by a higher grade level of support person than phone support. Online chat seems to be faster than traditional phone support. There are no language barriers to overcome.

WEBSITE FAQs and COMMON PROBLEMS

Check the web and the COMMON PROBLEMS AND SOLUTIONS and the FAQ sections in detail.

EMAIL

Email is probably the slowest help method but may be advisable if the problem doesn't require a quick turnaround response.

OTHER SUPPORT METHODS

Most people are aware of traditional forms of computer help - calling the manufacturer, checking the website, calling a computer reseller or bugging a friend or family member. Here are some other alternatives that may help to solve a computer problem:

- REMOTE POLLING
- ONLINE USER GROUPS
- LOCAL USER GROUPS

1. REMOTE SUPPORT OPTION

A growing trend in the computer industry is remote takeover of a computer over the Internet to run an online diagnostic to repair computer problems. A support person in some cases can run a program and gain access to a computer. The service person can then remotely take over the system and attempt to repair the problem. Remote polling can be a method to get help, if the option is available.

Software must be installed on the computer to be supported. You must give the person attempting to connect to your computer access. A remote log in service such as LOGMEIN will be used.

This is usually a pay for the service method, so make sure that the service is legitimate. The service usually is a Scam if the service contacts the user.

Remote polling does have limitations. This option only works if the remote computer can connect to the computer and if the computer doesn't start Windows, the remote polling option won't work.

2. ONLINE or LOCAL USER GROUPS

An online user group is any group that meets on the web or locally to discuss a particular topic. These groups can be very interesting and helpful. To find an online group for a particular computer or problem, Google the computer or problem and type GROUP or DISCUSSION GROUP after and see where the search leads.

Google and Yahoo have their groups and may be a good place to start. Read the group rule prior to diving right in to ask a question. Would you walk into a strange house amidst a group of total strangers and ask for help on your problem? Keep that in mind prior to "invading" an online discussion.

TIPS FOR WORKING WITH ONLINE or LOCAL USER GROUPS

1. Check the history.
2. Be polite.
3. Be humble.

CHECK THE HISTORY

There is a chance that your particular problem has been discussed already. Check any history or FAQ files. It's possible the answer can be obtained without initiating contact with the group. Before crashing a user group, read some of the questions and responses. Make sure that you're in an appropriate online spot to get proper help.

MIND YOUR MANNERS

Be nice and polite. Screaming at the person attempting to help does no one any good and you don't want to get hung up on.

The key to solving computer problems isn't so much knowing the answer, but knowing HOW to get the answer.

36. USING A COMPUTER SERVICE DEPARTMENT

Heaven forbid if you have to resort to using a computer department; however, if so here are some tips:

TYPE OF SERVICE CENTER

As a consumer I prefer smaller shops in general and would use a smaller computer shop that specializes in computer service. The larger electronic chain stores generally price most repairs higher hoping to switch a consumer to a new system instead of having to perform service work.

Smaller shops are usually more focused on solving the problem, will only suggest a replacement as a last resort and probably charge less for the repair than the larger appliance stores.

PRIOR TO SERVICE CHECK-IN

1. BACKUP DATA

If possible, copy all important files on a flash drive or external hard drive. If Windows doesn't start, attempt running in Safe Mode to save data. If possible, backup the MY DOCUMENTS and any other important data.

QuickBooks, TurboTax and other programs require data backup within the particular program and not through Windows. Inform the service people at the counter upon check in whether data is backed up and what files are important. Verify that "information or data important" is noted on the service work order.

Inform the service person that your files are very important and not to do anything to remove them without first discussing with you. Make sure that FILES IMPORTANT is written somewhere on the service work order.

2. WRITE DOWN or PRINT OUT ANY ERROR MESSAGES

Specific error messages can be helpful to a tech department, for example "Data Error reading drive C" gives a tech an idea of the problem.

3. ONLY TAKE NECESSARY ITEMS TO THE SERVICE CENTER

Desktop computers only require the base unit unless the problem is video display related or the desktop has a special connection AC power cord. If the problem is video related, bring the monitor. The tech should be able to isolate the problem at the counter. If the problem is monitor related, don't check in the computer, and purchase a replacement monitor. If the problem is not wireless related, remove any wireless USB network adapters from the computer.

Don't leave a mouse, keyboard, monitor or power cord unless requested. Bring all CDs and DVDs including any backup set of recovery DVDs. Make you're your last name is on the DVD covers or any USB flash drives. The service department should not check in anything they don't require working on the system; however you want to make sure that you get back everything left. Make sure ALL left items are documented on the service work order.

4. CHECK-IN THE NOTEBOOK POWER SUPPLY

Label and check-in the AC charger being used with the notebook. The AC charger may be defective and be the cause of the problem. Check in the notebook with a bag if the service department will accept it. The bag will protect the notebook. If the service department does take the bag, empty the bag of any non-essential items. We usually don't accept notebook bags on check-in because it's just another item that we have to take bailment of and could possibly lose.

5. LABEL ALL ITEMS

It's not a bad idea to take masking tape and place your name and phone number on your system, monitor, power supply, DVDs or any other item being left with the service center.

QUESTIONS TO ASK AT THE CHECK-IN COUNTER

1. DO YOU HAVE EXPERIENCE REPAIRING THIS PROBLEM?

Ask CAN YOU REPAIR IT? If they don't have experience with the problem you're wasting money. On the other hand, they may have experience with the problem and may tell you up front that the problem may not be affordably correctable so money isn't wasted checking in a system that won't be approved for repair anyway.

2. WHAT IS THE APPROXIMATE REPAIR COST?

Most service centers should be able to give an estimate based on the problem and have a price listing of repair costs. It may be possible to pre-approve certain repair and repair costs, to avoid phone tag and possibly get the system back quicker. Avoid any shop that charges on an hourly rate and doesn't cap a repair at a fixed cost.

3. DOES THE DIAGNOSITIC FEE APPLY TOWARD THE REPAIR?

Most service centers have a minimum check-in diagnostic charge. Ask if the upfront diagnostic fee applies TOWARDS THE REPAIR or is it a diagnostic fee only. We charge an upfront $59 diagnostic fee that applies toward a completed repair, data save or system replacement if necessary.

Some stores may have a service center that is mandated to push customers toward replacing equipment, instead of repairing and a diagnostic fee that doesn't apply towards a repair is an indication of that type of shop.

4. HOW LONG BEFORE THE SYSTEM GETS DIAGNOSED?

Notice the word DIAGNOSED, not repaired. The system has to be diagnosed before it can be repaired. The key is to get the computer diagnosed as quickly as possible, so a decision can be made on whether to get the computer repaired.

If the computer repair requires a replacement part that isn't in stock, the part needs to be ordered, which will delay the repair. The system needs to be tested once the repair is completed.

5. ARE EXPEDITED SERVICES OR LOANERS AVAILABLE?

If the repair estimate is too long, ask about expedited services or loaner equipment. The extra cost for a rental or faster service may be worth it if downtime is critical.

6. SAVING THE DATA

Make the check-in person aware if the data is important. There may be an extra charge to save data. Make the repair shop aware what data is most important. Make sure that DATA IMPORTANT is written or checked on the service work order.

7. IS THE WORK GUARANTEED?

Ask about the repair center's warranty on completed service work. A part replaced should have a hardware warranty. If Windows was re-installed, the warranty may only be 20-20 – Twenty steps out the door or 20 minutes, whichever comes first. Every shop is different, ask and check that there is nothing posted on the signed work order that contradicts what you are being told.

8. READ THE WORK ORDER FORM

Read what you're signing on check-in. The usual disclaimers in writing on the work order form include no responsibility for lost data and disposal of equipment not picked up within a certain period of time. Understand what you are agreeing to.

HARDWARE WARRANTY SERVICE

Let's assume that a computer that needs a hardware repair and the repair is covered under manufacturer warranty. We have good news and bad news:

THE GOOD NEWS

The computer should get repaired or replaced with very little cost to the owner.

THE BAD NEWS

The manufacturer warranty repair process for computers can be someplace between Hurricane Katrina and the BP spill in terms of how quickly the repair will be completed.

WARRANTY ESSENTIALS

A computer gets repaired or replaced under warranty coverage because the computer suffered hardware failure during the warranty period. The warranty period begins on the invoice purchase date and expires on the date as per the coverage agreement. Warranty repair for computers is handled by the manufacturer or a manufacturer authorized repair center unless an in-store extended warranty was purchased.

WARRANTY COVERAGE

Most manufacturer warranties cover a failure of the hardware components during the warranty period. New products usually have a one year manufacturer warranty.

Manufacturer REFURBISHED products usually have a 90 day warranty. The manufacturer should either repair or replace any defective component without cost to the consumer under the warranty period.

WARRANTY EXCLUSIONS

Warranty exclusion is something the manufacturer won't repair free. Most manufacturers won't cover a beer spill in or drop of a notebook. Usually physical trauma to a computer falls under the category of User Caused and is not covered under normal warranty. It's important to read the warranty exclusions for both the original warranty and any warranty extension.

EXTENDED WARRANTY COVERAGE

An extended warranty is warranty coverage beyond the original warranty period. If the computer has a one year manufacturer warranty, an extended warranty extends the original manufacturer coverage from one to three years. The extended warranty can be provided by the original manufacturer or a third party. Refer to the chapter on extended warranties for additional information.

THE WARRANTY PROCESS

There are three steps to get a computer repaired though manufacturer's warranty process:

1. Get the RMA authorization to send the computer back for repair.
2. Return the computer for repair.
3. Receive the system and test the system to check that the problem was indeed fixed.

1. THE RMA

To get the RMA (Return Merchandise Authorization) from the manufacturer is the first and largest hurdle. The RMA is process is necessary to get the manufacturer to give authorization to send the computer back for evaluation of problem and repair. Be prepared to be on hold, disconnected and generally given the run-around. Be patient and persistent. Have the following information available when making first contact for the RMA:

- Original purchase invoice.
- Copy of credit card receipt.
- Make model and serial number of the unit.
- Nature of the problem.

First check where the computer was purchased and if possible attempt to get a written diagnostic from the store. If our store sold a manufacturer-warranted computer that needs warranty work, we will complete a service work order stating the nature of the problem, which will make it easier for the customer to get an RMA issued for product return.

The customer has to jump through fewer hoops if they have a diagnostic stating the problem is hardware related. The repair center will not reimburse for the diagnostic; however, the RMA should be issued without much resistance.

Be prepared to follow the support person's instructions. Ask for a call back number if case the phone call gets disconnected. The service rep may ask to turn on the computer and get into the SETUP utility to run hardware diagnostics.

Follow their instructions and assuming the problem is hardware related an RMA number, which gives permission to return the computer for repair. Get an estimate of the turnaround time to plan how long you'll be without a system.

Avoid having the support person shipping out a replacement part and walking you through a part installation. An end-user should not be responsible for repairing their in-warranty system.

Instead ask them sending a tech out to perform the hardware replacement. If they don't, ask to speak to a supervisor. If still no satisfaction, tell the company that you plan to file a complaint to the online BBB. Manufacturers hate having to respond to a BBB letter.

2. RETURNING THE SYSTEM FOR REPAIR

Assuming the authorized repair center isn't local and the system has to be shipped, follow the listed steps to properly return a computer for repair:

TAKE PICTURES

Take photos of the item being returned prior to boxing. Send a copy along with the item. This is proof of the physical condition of the computer prior to shipping. This eliminates the possible warranty exclusion excuse that the problem was damage caused by the user.

DATA

Make the service representative aware and note that data is important on the work order. Most companies will not guarantee data on any computer returned for warranty repair. Take the computer to a local repair shop to have important files saved from the hard drive prior to sending the computer in for service.

BOX PROPERLY

If you kept the original boxes and packing, use them for packing. Have the RMA number as part of the ship to address. Box and pack carefully. Only send back what the repair facility requests. If the computer is a desktop, there is no reason to send the LCD, mouse, keyboard or power cord unless specifically requested by the manufacturer. Send the charger with a notebook and double box for extra protection.

ENCLOSE A SHORT NOTE

Place a short note along with the unit stating the make, model and RMA return number, serial number of the unit with a brief description of the problem. Send a copy of the original purchase receipt and make copies of all the paperwork.

SHIP INSURED

Ship by an insured carrier that providing tracking and signed proof of delivery.

3. RECEIVING THE REPLACEMENT

Check and note any exterior box damage prior to opening the box. After opening check the serial number of the unit. Is the same computer back or was it replaced? Check for any physical damage. Turn it on and check to verify that the problem was corrected. If the repair took a long period of time, ask about a warranty extension to at least cover the period of time you were without the unit because it was out for repair.

WHILE THE COMPUTER IS IN SERVICE

RENTALS

A computer rental is a specialty market. Consumers pay a premium for any rental product and a computer is no exception. Consider spending a couple of hundred dollars and purchase a used 2nd computer or netbook. Rentals normally do not include Microsoft Office so ask what pre-installed programs come installed on the system rental.

SQUEAKY WHEEL STRATEGY

Yelling, screaming and cursing may actually hurt your cause. If I'm in a restaurant and have a problem with the food served, I politely discuss the problem with the server.

One doesn't want the server telling the cook in the back that some jerk is complaining. While my techs haven't spat on any customers' computers; however, I'm sure there are techs out there that have on occasion taken longer on a chronic complainer's system.

COMPUTER TECH ANNOYANCES

Listed below are computer tech pet peeves:

1. CHECK IN THE NOTEBOOK AC ADAPTER CORD IN KNOTS

A tech gets annoyed when they have to spend a couple minutes unknotting a notebook power cord. The technician is thinking one of two things:

- "How did it get like this?"
- "This jerk has no respect for his equipment."

2. PERFORM SPRING CLEANING OF A COMPUTER ON THE SERVICE COUNTER

If the computer is dirty when disconnecting it at home, clean it there. It's amazing the number of people that decide to clean their computer right on the service counter. How would you react if a stranger entered your house and wiped their dirty shoes on your rug after entering your home?

3. LEAVE A SUGGESTIVE BACKGROUND PICTURE ON THE DESKTOP

If possible, remove any suggestive screen backgrounds and replace it with a blank background or something less suggestive. Nudie screen savers and background images are tacky.

4. ASK NON-RELATED "HOW TO" QUESTIONS

Nothing annoys a tech more than asking the tech to tell them how to do something un-related to the repair. Training time is billed separately and in addition to repairing a problem.

5. ASK ABOUT BEING BONDED BECAUSE THEIR INFORMATION IS SO IMPORTANT

Most techs really don't care what's on a system. Making a comment like that is an invitation for every tech in the place to review everything on the hard drive. FYI computer service techs aren't held to the same level of client confidentiality as priests, doctors and lawyers.

If the information is so important that the repair shop has to be bonded, take it down the local FBI office to get worked on or have it done in-house with company techs.

6. THE DATA IS IMPORTANT, BUT NOT SURE WHAT DATA EXACTLY

The tech loves that customer because the dollar meter is running. The tech isn't responsible to tell you what data is important. That conversation shouldn't be necessary if the data was backed up in the first place.

7. SHOW UP 5 MINUTES PRIOR TO CLOSING AND ASK THAT THE COMPUTER BE SETUP TO VERIFY THAT THE PROBLEM IS CORRECTED

The request to check out the system prior to pick up isn't unreasonable; however, do not show up at quitting time.

8. CALLING THE REPAIR CENTER BACK 6 MONTHS AFTER PICK UP COMPLAINING THAT THE COMPUTER NEVER WORKED RIGHT OR ASKING FOR FREE HELP ON A TOTALLY UNRELATED TOPIC

We make follow-up calls to every customer a couple of days after picking up their system. We call to verify that their computer is working properly so they can't use that "it never worked right since I picked it up" or "I know I picked it up two months ago, but I'm just setting it up and just noticed the problem wasn't fixed". Does anyone believe that?

Use these tips to get the maximum benefits using a service center.

37. ONSITE SERVICE

When we receive calls for on-site service, in most cases we attempt to talk the caller out of an on-site call, which surprises most callers. The main reason we discourage on-site computer repair is that the customer is going to pay significantly more for a job that won't be done as well.

THE PRICE OF CONVENIENCE

People are stressed and don't have the time needed to research and repair a computer problem and can't be bothered to:

- Disconnect the computer.
- Load it into the car.
- Drive it to the computer store.
- Wait for the repair to be completed.
- Pick it back up.
- Take it home.
- Reconnect everything.
- Reload the programs and restore the data.

ON-SITE SERVICE ADVANTAGES

An on-site computer service call is the ultimate in consumer convenience. The on-site customer doesn't have to disconnect their computer or drive it to a service center. They don't have to carry the computer down the steps, into the car and into the shop. The technician works on the computer while the onsite service customer goes about their business, perform house chores or watch TV. There are times when on-site computer service is preferable to taking a computer to a service center.

WHEN TO USE ON-SITE SERVICE

HOME NETWORK OR HOME THEATRE / SECURITY SETUP

A home network is when the computers will share files and information through Windows. A home network setup can be complicated and may require a technician. Understand the difference between setting up a home network and making sure that multiple computers in the home have Internet access.

To setup multiple computers for the Internet is just a matter of giving each computer access to the Internet through the high speed modem through a wireless router or through cables. Understand the differences and your requirements. Most homes only want multiple computers to have Internet access.

More sophisticated home theatre or home security setups can be involved. When large televisions or cameras have to be mounted a service technician familiar with the equipment may be required.

THE COMPUTER CANNOT BE PHYSICALLY MOVED

Many seniors want on-site service because of their physical limitations or they are just not comfortable disconnecting the cables and are afraid that they may not be capable of reconnecting the computer. Place tape on and label each connection port prior to disconnecting. Seniors prefer notebooks because notebooks are smaller, easier to move and have fewer connections to worry about.

DISADVANTAGES OF ON-SITE SERVICE

On average an on-site service call may cost 2-3 times the amount for the same repair if the computer was taken to a shop. The user pays a premium for the convenience.

The repair won't be done as well if the system was taken to a service center because the on-site technician has two limited resources: equipment and time. The follow examples show why on-site service should not be used in certain cases:

EXAMPLE 1: COMPUTER INFECTED WITH VIRUSES AND SPYWARE

No single virus protection program removes every virus, spyware and malware file. We run complete scans with up to 8 different virus, spyware and malware removal programs. Each program may take anywhere from 30 minutes to hours to run depending on conditions.

Once the scans are completed, the computer then has to be tested. We spend time with the computer on the Internet to make sure that the computer doesn't get re-infected.

Assuming that problem is corrected, the computer usually requires Windows updates and an optimization. That's an extra hour to a day depending on conditions. Do the math. It takes a day to properly repair a virused computer. Not many onsite companies are going to spend a day on any one call.

QUESTIONS TO ASK THE ON-SITE COMPANY ON VIRUS / SPYWARE REMOVAL

1. How do charge for a virus and spyware removal? By the hour or by the job?
2. How many removal programs are run?
3. Is the repair cost capped? If they quote and work on the clock, look for a different service option.
4. How is the computer tested?
5. Is the work warranted?

EXAMPLE 2: WINDOWS RE-INSTALLATION

A proper Windows re-installation takes a day to complete. The initial Window reload may take only up to an hour to complete, but getting all additional Windows updates can take hours to days to completely update a computer.

Assuming the re-installation went well, all non-Windows programs have to be installed and the computer has to be tested. If data is important, data first has to be saved prior to a Windows re-installation. If Windows doesn't start properly, the hard drive may have to be pulled for the data save.

QUESTIONS TO ASK THE ON-SITE COMPANY REGARDING A WINDOWS RE-INSTALLATION:

1. How do you treat a Windows re-installation? By the hour or by the job?
2. Is the repair cost capped? Again, look for a company that quotes by the job, not by the hour.
3. Does the quoted installation price include retrieving and installing Windows Updates?
4. Is the work warranted?
5. Will I lose my data or programs?

Most on-site service companies only restore the original version of Windows without getting updates to save time. This incomplete process leaves an older version of Windows on the system, which is more vulnerable to virus and hacker attacks.

EXAMPLE 3 – HARDWARE PROBLEM

What if the part needed is proprietary to that particular computer and the on-site tech doesn't have a replacement? If the problem is with a power supply, the power outage may have caused a secondary problem with Windows? What if the problem is a bad motherboard? A bad motherboard usually cannot be repaired on site. Or the system has viruses or spyware. What if data has to be saved?

If using an on-site company for a possible hardware problem:

- Get a repair cost estimate.
- Make sure they know the make and model of the computer.
- Ask about the cost if the system isn't affordably repairable.

PICKUP DROPOFF SERVICE

If the system can't be repaired on-site, ask the tech if the computer can be taken back to the service center, repaired and returned. This method offers the best of both worlds – the full service capability of a repair shop with the convenience of in-home pickup and drop-off service.

On-site service should be only be used to setup a home network or if a person is physically unable to move a computer.

38. COMPUTER TRAINING

TAKING CLASSES VERSUS USING A DEDICATED TRAINER

One hour of individual training should be of more benefit than a half a dozen training classes in a class with other people. Class time is wasted by other people in the class asking questions, many of which will not be relevant to your situation.

TRAINING LOCATION

If you own a notebook you don't need a trainer to come to your residence. Meet at a coffee shop, library or anywhere other than your home.

If the trainer is coming to your home, make sure to thoroughly check references prior to allowing a stranger in your home even for computer training. It may not be a bad idea to have a friend over during the initial training for safety reasons. At least have them "sit in" for the first ten minutes or so.

YOU WANT TO CONTROL THE SESSION

Direct the trainer on what to cover and not vice versa. Many trainers like to talk a lot to show off their wealth of knowledge. They may go off topic and begin to cover material that may not be as much use to you.

Find out if the trainer can address your needs prior to the appointment. Make a list of questions and review them with the trainer <u>prior</u> to the appointment. By giving the trainer a preview of your issues, the trainer can be prepared to address your needs as efficiently as possible. If your main concern is sending and receiving emails, make that issue as the number one priority and cover that first.

WINDOWS TUTORIALS

Windows has built in online tutorials and training that is useful. If you aren't sure how to transfer data to a USB flash drive, use the help and online tutorials within Windows. Enter whatever you would like to accomplish in the run command, such as "COPY A DVD" and the tutorial will walk you through how to do this. Try using the online help.

WINDOWS HELP AND TUTORIAL SCREENS

The person being trained should dictate or at least have some say on what is covered during the training session.

39. PRINTER REPAIRS & INK CARTRIDGE REFILLS

Our company repaired inkjet printers until the price on brand new inkjet printers dropped to $50 on up. We still get a person at least once a week that drags in a broken inkjet printer of manufacturer warranty.

I explain to the customer that it will cost at least $100 parts and labor to repair the printer and a brand new replacement printer with a one year warranty will cost $50 - $100. It just makes more sense to replace an inkjet printer in most situations.

COMMON INKJET PRINTER PROBLEM

Let's assume an out of warranty inkjet printer has a paper pickup problem. There is no physical paper jam to remove, so the paper pickup assembly has to be replaced.

Replacing a printer pickup roller shouldn't be a problem; just order the part and replace it. Except the part costs over $100! How can that be when a brand new printer with a one year warranty and cartridges initially cost $ 50 for the entire printer?

WHY INKJET PRINTERS ARE SO INEXPENSIVE

The printer manufacturers sell printers below cost to get their printers in the hands of as many consumers as possible. The printers are sold below cost because the printer manufacturers **make their profits on selling the replacement ink cartridge and toner refills.**

Consider the cost of a gallon of gasoline. During an extreme gas shortage, the gas price may shoot up to $4 to $5 per gallon.

A gallon of printer ink would cost thousands of dollars based on purchasing a gallon of ink to fill ink cartridge cartridges.

I knew one person that actually purchases a replacement printer every time his printer runs out of ink. That's a little extreme and not good for the landfill, but you get the point. Inkjet printers are cheap, the ink is expensive.

Some inkjet printers use up to seven separate cartridges. A user can spend $60-80 per set of ink replacement cartridges, which is almost the cost of a new inkjet printer.

LASER PRINTERS

A laser printer is more expensive than an inkjet printer. Lasers use toner, not ink to print. Toner is a powdery substance. Toner cost more than ink; however, each toner will print thousands of copies instead of the hundreds of copy output from a replacement ink refill.

The cost per printed page is much less with lasers. If you print over 50-100 copies a week, you may want to consider purchasing a laser printer. Lasers are used by businesses, than homeowners, but like every electronic item, prices have dropped on them.

If an inkjet or black and white only laser printer is out of warranty and replacing cartridge or toner doesn't correct the problem, REPLACE THE PRINTER. Get a repair estimate on a color laser printer repair only.

SAVE MONEY ON PRINTING

1. USE THIRD PARTY INK REFILLS

Third party ink cartridge refills are ink cartridges made by a party other than the printer manufacturer. Using non-manufacturer or refilled ink cartridges can save money on printing costs.

<u>Third party inks do not void a manufacturer warranty</u>. If the inkjet printer has a warranty issue and you are afraid that sending the printer with third party inks may void the warranty, remove the third party cartridges and re-place the cartridges with the manufacturer's cartridges back into the printer prior to getting the printer serviced.

Ink cartridge refills may not work as well or provide as many pages as manufacturer inks. Have an estimate of the number of pages your printer produces with printer manufacturer cartridges. Check the number of pages printed with remanufactured inks.

Remember it's the cost per page that determines what cartridge or toner is the best value. What good is less expensive ink cartridge if the print output drops significantly?

2. INK REFILL KITS

If you are brave and don't mind cleaning up a mess, purchase an ink refill kit and learn to refill your own cartridges. Expect to ruin at least 3-5 cartridges before you get the hang of it. Use a sink in the basement if possible. Watch a couple of how to videos on YouTube prior to attempting.

REMANUFACTURER VERSUS REFILLED INK CARTRIDGES

Remanufactured ink cartridges are cartridges filled by a company other than the original printer manufacturer. Ink refills are empty manufacturer cartridges that someone refills with ink using a syringe or an ink filling machine. We rarely bother filling cartridges in-house because we can purchase already filled cartridges online from companies that sell inexpensive cartridges.

Check locally for any ink cartridge refilling store or service. Today even drug stores and warehouse clubs offer ink refilling services. Search on eBay or GOOGLE on-line for the type of cartridge or toner your printer requires.

3. PRINT IN DRAFT MODE

Setup the printer to print in a lower quality mode to save on ink. Unless printing a final copy to send, print in lower quality mode. The output quality can be adjusted under the PRINTER settings in Control Panel.

4. RUN THE PRINTER CLEANING UTILITY

Run the printer head cleaning utility at least once every two weeks, even if the printer wasn't used. Running the printer head cleaning utility once a week should keep the printer ink from drying out.

If a printer cartridge dries out from non-use, remove the cartridge from the printer and run the cartridge under hot water for 2-3 seconds to loosen the ink. Keep water away from the metal sensors. It's a good idea to place masking tape over the metal sensors to prevent water damage, prior to running warm water on the ink ejection nozzles.

HOW TO CLEAR AN OBSTRUCTED INK CARTRIDGE

1. Cover the cartridge metal sensors with masking tape so the sensors don't get wet.
2. Run hot water over ink nozzles for 2-3 seconds.
3. Use a paper towel and blot the cartridge until ink begins to show on the paper towel. If ink appears, remove the masking tape and re-insert the cartridge back into the printer.
4. If ink doesn't appear on the paper towel after blotting, repeat the process another time.
5. If ink appears, wipe down the cartridge and replace back in the printer.

This process works very well on many different manufacturer cartridges. It does work better on the larger sized and older ink cartridges.

Run the printer cleaning process at least three consecutive times.

The cleaning process can be found under the printer SETTINGS in the printer menu. The cleaning process can be run within WINDOWS. Select CONTROL PANEL / DEVICES AND PRINTERS / Right Click on the PRINTER ICON / Select PROPERTIES / Search for the PRINT HEAD CLEANING UTILITY.

MOST COMMON INK CARTRIDGE PROBLEMS

1. **PRINTER INDICATES CARTRIDGES ARE EMPTY AFTER REPLACING A NEW REFILLED CARTRIDGE**

    If the printer indicates that there is an empty cartridge after replacing, power off the printer by removing the printer power cord from the wall, wait 10 seconds and then plug the cord back into the wall socket and turn everything back on. If the message continues repower again and attempt to print anyway. The printer was reset with the replacement cartridge and should now work.

    The printer should work. **PRINTER DOESN'T PRINT**

    - Make sure that all protective tape was removed from the cartridge.
    - Attempt a test print directly from the printer to determine if the problem is printer related or a problem with the computer printer connection interface.
    - Attempt to print a Windows test page to determine if the problem is with the printer or the application program attempting to print from.
    - Run hot water over the ink eject nozzles only.
    - Purchase a manufacturer cartridge to see if the problem is with the refilled cartridge.

2. **PRINTER DOESN'T RECOGNIZE THE CARTRIDGE**

    - Attempt to print anyway. The printer may still work.
    - Remove the cartridge, replace in the printer and try to print again.
    - Leave the cartridge in the printer and physically remove the printer power plug from the wall and replug. This type of printer reset is more effective than using the OFF-ON power button.
    - Finally repeat the above step and restart the computer and repower both devices with the cartridges installed. Resetting the printer and computer both and may correct the problem.

LASER PRINTERS

A laser printer may be a better option if printing at least 500 copies per month. Laser toners need to be replaced after thousands or copies, while ink cartridges are replaced after a couple of hundred pages. The cost per printed page is less with a laser printer.

Lasers are a much better value if only black print is required. Color lasers are more expensive and like inkjet printers, individual color toners need to be replaced when a color toner expires.

TONER VERSUS CARTRIDGE INK

Color laser printer toner cartridges are more expensive than ink cartridges, but their yield (number of printed pages per toner) is higher so the cost per printed page will be less expensive than an inkjet cartridge.

If printing requirements only include a few color copies per month, choose an inkjet printer. An inkjet printer can create beautiful photo prints at a much initial lower price. Keep in mind that the inexpensive price of an inkjet is quickly surpassed by the cost of replacement ink.

COMMON PRINTER PROBLEMS

Listed are some of the more common printing problems and solutions.

1. PAPER JAM

- Turn off the printer
- Open the printer doors
- Remove the paper input tray
- Pull out the sheets in the direction of the paper path. Do not pull out the paper against the flow of paper.

Use a heavy bonded paper and when refilling the paper tray to move the oldest paper in the tray to the top to use it first. Paper exposed to a humid environment will warp and jam more. Flip the paper constantly to keep it from warping sooner.

2. PRINT JOB IS STUCK IN THE PRINT QUE

Click the PRINTER ICON on the bottom right taskbar and delete all print jobs. Turn off and restart the printer, which should clear all print jobs.

3. DOCUMENTS PRINT GARBLED OR DON'T PRINT COMPLETELY

- Turn off the computer and printer, re-start both and attempt to re-print.
- Delete and re-install the printer driver.

4. NEED TO RE-INSTALL THE PRINTER DRIVER

- Use the CD that came with the printer
- If the computer doesn't have a CD drive, download the printer driver directly from the manufacturer's website.
- Windows may automatically setup the printer. Power up the printer prior to connecting the printer cable to the computer

PRINTER MAINTENANCE

INKJET PRINTERS

Inkjet printer maintenance is making sure to use the printer at least once a week to keep the printer ink from drying out and running the PRINTER CLEANING UTILITY under Control Panel at least once every couple of weeks. Run the printer maintenance option in Windows:

- Select CONTROL PANEL / PRINTER
- RIGHT CLICK on the Printer Icon and select PROPERTIES.
- Select MAINENANCE / Run the HEAD CLEANING Program.

LASER PRINTERS

A laser printer needs routine cleaning. Disconnect power to the printer and remove the toner cartridge prior to cleaning. Take the printer outside and compress clean the printer with a can of compressed air. Remove all toners and open all doors. Use the entire can.

PAPER FEED ROLLERS

Paper feed rollers are going to get dirty. Alcohol hardens the rollers and they won't grab paper as well. Use soapy water to clean the rollers.

Purchase a printer based off the on-going printing cost.

40. COMPUTERS AND THE ENVIRONMENT

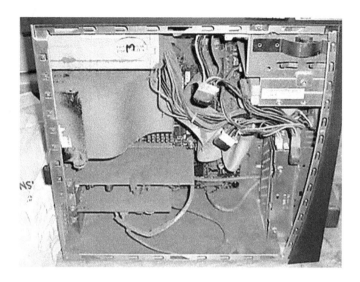

The above computer was the winner in our first annual "Cruddy Computer Case" contest. The owner allowed us to post it on YouTube only if we promised not to use her name or identify her in any way with this computer.

A computer can be affected by its surrounding environment. A computer will last longer and has less chance to malfunction if its environmental surroundings are friendly and more to its liking. Computers don't get along with dust, hairy pets, lightning, liquids, power surges, static, heat, cold and rough people (not necessarily in that order).

DUST

Dust is the computer's ultimate enemy. Computers act as a dust magnet and the power supply fan draws dust inside the desktop, not out. Dust builds up around the CPU, cooling fan and memory. Dust causes the components to overheat, the fan to run slower or stop spinning and either problem can cause the computer to overheat and shut down.

Once a year purchase a can of compressed air ($10), remove the computer side panel, and take the computer outside and compress clean. A good cleaning will take almost 5 minutes. Shoot the air both directions through the power supply and focus on the CPU and memory.

PETS

Animal hair can cause computers problems. The best way for computers and pets to co-exist is to close the door and deny a pet access to walking on the computer keyboard when there is no pet supervision.

POWER SURGES

A computer's parts are designed to operate within certain electrical parameters. A power spike or loss of power can cause a computer or other electronic equipment to fail.

LIMIT POWER SURGE PROBLEMS

- Don't use a computer during a lightning and thunder storm.
- Disconnect the computer from the wall during a lightning and thunder storm.
- Use a surge protector that has a minimum 1200 Joule rating.

LIQUIDS

Liquids and computers don't mix. A liquid spill on a desktop keyboard is a $10-20 replacement part. A liquid spill on a notebook keyboard may ruin the keyboard, motherboard or both.

Place any liquid behind a notebook screen, not on the side. By placing the drink BEHIND the screen, it can't fall forward or sideways onto the notebook.

AIR FLOW

Don't use a notebook on a bed where the air flow is restricted. Get a notebook cooling pad to place underneath the notebook. The cooling pad will blow air into the notebook, allowing it to run cooler.

The above illustration is a notebook pad cooler. The notebook or laptop rests on top and the fans blow air in the notebook bottom, helping to keep it cool. The fan is powered by a USB connection that plugs into the notebook.

HEAT, COLD & HUMIDITY

Computers don't like temperature extremes. If a notebook was in the truck of a car overnight, wait at least one hour to turn on the notebook, in order for the components to warm up prior to use.

STATIC ELECTRICITY

Static electricity doesn't mix with computers. To fight static electricity:

- Place a static free mat for your feet in the work area.
- Touch metal prior to working with a computer to dissipate the static within your body.

DISCARDING EQUIPMENT

Please don't throw out any broken LCD monitors or computers. It's illegal. Check locally to see where to properly dispose of unwanted broken computer equipment. Usually the local Goodwill store will accept unwanted electronics. If Goodwill will not accept the equipment, check with the local solid waste authority about local recycling events.

RECYCLE COMPUTERS, CARTRIDGES AND TONERS

Printer manufacturers and resellers may sell toner cartridges at a discount to customers that return the empty cartridges for recycling. This is to partially discourage customers from refilling the cartridges and to help to save the environment.

Manufacturers have programs for recycling their inkjet and toner cartridges. Check with your local non-profits to see if they accept computer equipment for recycling. Some non-profits will accept donated equipment and send off to manufacturers for proper recycling. Most states will offer recycling days where consumers can drop off their unwanted electronics.

DATA ON HARD DRIVES

If you are concerned about leaving information on a computer being recycled, either remove the data or physically remove the hard drive prior to recycling. Don't expect the donation center to remove data.

Take proper care of the computer and recycle properly to preserve the environment.

41. EXTENDED WARRANTIES

An extended warranty extends the hardware warranty coverage on an item. The extended coverage includes defective hardware only. Coverage not included with most extended warranties:

- Software problems (viruses / spyware / Windows reloads)
- User abuse (Such as dropping a notebook and cracking the screen)
- Power problems (check with the warranty provider)

EXTENDED WARRANTY COVERAGE QUESTIONS

Some questions to ask when deciding whether to accept or decline an extended warranty:

1. WHO IS PROVIDING THE COVERAGE?

Who is providing the warranty coverage - the manufacturer or a third party? If the warranty is provided by the store and the store goes out of business, extended warranty coverage is worthless.

If the warranty is through a national third party provider, the consumer will have to deal directly with the warranty company and their service center. Consider a computer warranty service as similar to dealing with an insurance company. The issue should get resolved, but not in a fast time frame.

2. COVERAGE IS FROM WHEN TO WHEN?

On used equipment, we offer warranties extending from 30 days to 90 days or one year. Most extended third party warranties overlap the manufacturer warranty the first year, so a two year or three year warranty extension is really only a one or two year extension. Understand the coverage prior to purchasing.

3. WHAT ARE THE EXCLUSIONS?

Normal warranties have exclusions for what they call "user abuse". Coverage typically doesn't include screen damage from drops or liquid spills onto the notebook. Know in advance what IS NOT covered.

4. IS THE WARRANTY TRANSFERRABLE?

Specific warranties may be transferrable to a second user. Dell allows a warranty transfer; however, an online transfer must be completed. A transferrable warranty is a definite benefit to selling a used computer.

IS AN EXTENDED WARRANTY WORTH IT?

It depends on whether you believe in extended warranties or not. Consider the extended warranty on large screen televisions if service is done in-home. Who wants to take a 52in plasma LCD off a wall and transport it to a repair shop?

If the warranty is under $100 for an additional two years of coverage for a notebook, purchase it. Check that coverage doesn't overlap or is not concurrent with an existing manufacturer warranty.

COMPREHENSIVE WARRANTY COVERAGE

Certain warranty coverage now includes repair or replacement even if the computer or notebook is physically damaged by user negligence. Comprehensive coverage can cover liquid spills, drops, cracked screens and other types of damage or trauma not normally covered by basic warranty coverage. Comprehensive coverage will cost more but may be worth it if someone in the household has the dropsies.

SQUARE TRADE

Square Trade is currently the best third party warranty company in the electronics industry. Square Trade will cover most new items and some refurbished items. New items can be extended from one to three years and manufacturer refurbished items can be extended to one year.

Square Trade warranty pricing is typically less expensive than appliance store extended warranty pricing and they handle warranty claims in a timely, fair manner. Check out Square trade at sqaretrade.com.

MAINTENANCE PLANS

A maintenance plan is similar to a retainer fee or insurance plan for a computer. A business or individual pays a standard monthly or yearly fee to a computer repair individual or business in exchange for computer service and support.

A maintenance plan can be slightly different from an extended warranty in that maintenance plans may cover on-site service and software repairs. The individual or business in turn will provide computer help when the maintenance plan holder has a computer problem.

The help can either be provided on-site, over the Internet of over the phone. Any help provided may be covered under the plan or a discounted rate may apply. Each plan varies based off the company providing the plan and service. Many businesses take advantage of maintenance plans. Businesses benefit under a maintenance plan because the coverage includes on-site or expedited service.

Know who provides the extended warranty coverage, when it starts, expires, is it transferrable and the warranty exclusions.

42. MANUFACTURER SUPPORT

A support call has to be made to the manufacturer. Good Luck! Turn on the speaker phone and have the Google language translator website ready. Some helpful hints:

1. PREPARE FOR THE CALL EMOTIONALLY

Understand that this experience will be painful and prepare emotionally. Get in that frame of mind prior to making the call. Think of this as sitting down to do taxes except it probably won't cost as much.

2. PREPARE PHYSICALLY

Prior to the phone call do the following:

- Make a potty stop before making the call.
- Have water, coffee, and a snack of choice available.
- Have the TV on with remote in hand or internet device for surfing while on hold.
- Have the computer on (if it works).
- Have a piece of paper and pencil ready for notes.

3. GATHER THE FOLLOWING INFORMATION

- Copy of purchase receipt.
- Credit card payment receipt
- Credit card information in case the call is chargeable.
- Computer model number and serial number.
- The system hardware configuration (processor speed, amount of memory and free hard drive space).
- Any add-on devices.
- Any third party hardware and software information, including:
  1. Product name.
  2. Company name.
  3. Version number of product.
- Nature of the problem and what steps have been taken to fix the problem.
- A written paper copy of data or error messages.

4. ATTEMPT TO CALL DURING OFF PEAK HOURS

This may not be possible based on your schedule, but try to make this call during off peak business hours or service hours (weekends or Monday through Friday 9:00am to 5 pm). Try calling early in the morning or late in the evening during the week. Evenings and weekends are the worst time because the call volume is greater and the companies have fewer people manning the phones.

5. UNDERSTAND THE PROCESS

Assume that it may be awhile before actually speaking with a tech that can actually help. Most services companies have different levels of support people. Most service calls begin with a Level One support representative in training and if necessary the process will move to a higher level if the first tech cannot solve the problem.

Most support reps work from a script. The less experienced support staff requires a script to move the problem forward. Many companies will elevate the call to a more experienced person (Level 2) after a certain time period and the problem is still unresolved. Certain companies keep the call with the same support representative until either the problem is resolved or the call is terminated. Phone support can be a frustrating experience.

HELPFUL TIPS

1. BE CALM AND PATIENT

It's not easy for the support person either. Make it easier for both parties by just remaining calm. Don't get wound up drinking coffee prior to making that support call.

2. GET A CALL BACK NUMBER

Ask if there is any way to get a direct call back number in case the call gets disconnected. It can be painful to get disconnected and have to re-start the process from the beginning with a different rep.

3. FOCUS AND LISTEN TO THE QUESTION

Most computer tech support is farmed out overseas and the support person may speak with an accent. Ask the person to speak slower if you're having a problem understanding them.

Listen to the questions and answer the question. Stay focused and on point. Assume that in 10 minutes either the call will get disconnected or the problem will be solved.

4. WRITE IT DOWN

Take notes. Get the support person's name, badge number and other relevant information.

5. BE SURE TO HAVE A NEXT STEP RESOLUTION

If the problem isn't solved, make sure to understand the next step to solve the problem. Have the support rep commit to what is to happen next to get the problem solved and they are specific.

6. CAPTURE A SCREEN AND EMAIL

It's easier for a service representative to view a computer screen instead of you attempting to explain what they are seeing. To capture a screen image:

1. Press the PrtScn button to copy the screen to the clipboard.
2. Press the Windows Key+PrtScn buttons on the keyboard to save the screen to a file.
3. Use the built-in Snipping Tool.

To receive better service and support from a computer company, fill out the warranty registration information as a BUSINESS rather than an INDIVIDUAL.

When purchasing a computer, fill out contact information for warranty service. Input the warranty information as a business. Make up a business name and give correct information for everything else. If they ask to complete a survey, make the company aware that you may be purchasing additional equipment within the next year. Business accounts tend to get a better level of service than home buyers, so be smart and take advantage of that knowledge.

OTHER SUPPORT TIPS

1. DON'T GET CAUGHT IN THE MIDDLE

Don't get into a finger pointing situation where the vendor tries to push the problem off elsewhere. Usually if the problem is a non-internet access issue and the ISP can "ping" or send a signal to the computer, the problem is with the computer and not the service.

Eliminate finger pointing before the phone call. If the problem is internet connectivity with a device, use the device on other services. Use multiple devices on the service. Don't give the support person a reason to blow you off.

2. ESCALATE IF NECESSARY

If the person attempting to help is not helping, ask to escalate to a higher level person or get the problem escalated.

3. USE A PHONE WITH A HEADSET

A phone with a headset will free both hands for typing or moving things around as per the support person's instructions.

4. LOG THE CALL

Have a pen and paper to make notes of the call including person's name, badge number, date and time of the call and other pertinent information.

When calling the manufacturer for help be prepared and patient. Have something to do to pass the time while on hold.

43. 50 COMPUTER TIPS

1. Every manufacturer on a new system purchase must give provide a method for reinstalling Windows on the computer. LEARN THE METHOD FOR YOUR COMPUTER AND HOW TO USE IT.
2. When setting up equipment, allow at least 3" clearance from the wall so the computer fan can circulate air freely.
3. Avoid eating, drinking or smoking by computer equipment.
4. Keep your desktop organized and uncluttered. Place similar type files into FOLDERS for storage.
5. DO NOT PLUG OR UNPLUG any cables to or from the computer with the power on.
6. Never force connectors into place.
7. Don't tighten monitor connection cable screws too tight. It will be hard to unscrew them.
8. ALWAYS BACKUP important information to hard drive AND separate backup media such as flash drive, USB external hard drive, CD, OR online using the cloud OR both.
9. Alternate backup media (EX. - Use two different flash drives or DVD media and alternate for each backup). Constantly save any important file being worked on.
10. Backup information while working on a file at least every 10 minutes when working on the computer.
11. When changing system settings, write down the settings prior to changing to change back to the original settings if necessary.
12. Have all equipment connected to a surge protector that provides dollar compensation it the equipment is damaged by an electrical spike.
13. Do not force a USB plug into the connection on the system. If the USB device does not plug in, flip the USB device and attempt again.
14. Scan any files downloaded from a personal web-site for viruses prior to loading them on a computer.

15. Select the default options settings selected by the program when installing software.
16. When downloading a "free" program, use the "CUSTOM" download option instead of "EXPRESS" download, which will probably place multiple programs onto the computer.
17. Write down all program license codes and store them in a safe place.
18. Open MY PC OR MY COMPUTER and view the icons PRIOR to inserting a flash drive or external backup drive in the computer USB port. Note the drive letter Windows assigns for each new device for data transfer.
19. If it isn't broke, don't fix it. Refrain from making drastic changes to a working computer.
20. Keep all sales documents and boxes in case equipment has to be shipped for warranty service.
21. Write down serial numbers and tech support phone numbers and post them by the computer along with the system configuration.
22. Create a folder on the desktop and call it DOWNLOADS. Download all files from the Internet into this folder, so all downloaded files can be easily found.
23. Find the device drivers for the specific system online at the manufacturer's website and bookmark that page in case there is ever need to re-download the drivers.
24. Create a backup copy of all device drivers and store them off the system.
25. Label everything taken to a service department – CDs, notebook power chargers, anything that can be lost or misplaced, so the service center can match the missing part to the system.
26. Turn off all power management and sleep mode. Sleep mode causes more problems than it solves. Computers can enter sleep mode and take minutes to recover or not come back from sleep mode at all.
27. Create a restore point on the system prior to installing any major upgrade or change.
28. Do not remove a flash drive or external device from a computer until it can be safely removed from the computer as per the software. On the bottom right of the taskbar, RIGHT CLICK on the flash drive icon and Select SAFELY REMOVE HARDWARE.
29. A crashed PC may explain the reason for the crash in a cryptic message. Write down the message or if possible capture a screenshot. Research the error message on Google or provide the information to technical support.
30. If you are a solitaire player, solitaire and other games can be downloaded free of charge at the Microsoft website.
31. When cleaning a monitor or notebook LCD use a specialty LCD glass cleaner or just water, not glass cleaner.
32. Make sure to setup a backup Restore Point on a Windows computer.
33. Have multiple web browsers installed on each computer. If one web browser doesn't work, open a different browser to determine if the problem is with the web browser being used or a problem with the computer or Internet service itself.

34. Experiment with CORTANA for using your voice to command the computer, however phase in voice activation. Initially your primary use should be the good old fashioned mouse and keyboard.
35. Keyboard shortcut to open the task manager (Ctrl + Shift + Esc) and head to the startup tab to configure what programs to launch with the system.
36. To get a partial screen image shot in Windows: Windows: Select START and select SNIPPING TOOL.
37. Download and use VLC for playing almost any file.
38. Use NINITE for free software downloads.
39. Facebook has a powerful search engine so use it on occasion. One can use Facebook to enter a phone number to access a person's name.
40. Social networking sites are setup to share information. For example a video posted on YouTube can automatically be placed on Facebook, Twitter, Google Plus and Pinterest.
41. Make a backup RESTORE POINT PRIOR to making any major change to a system.
42. Do not remove a flash drive from a computer unless the computer is powered off or make sure the drive is safe to remove through software by clicking on the flash drive icon on the bottom right of the task bar and selecting "EJECT".
43. Do not leave open ink jet cartridges in a printer over an extended period of time (meaning months).
44. If donating or giving a computer to another user, make sure to do a FACTORY RECOVERY and wipe all information off the hard drive prior to giving it.
45. Make sure to remove all tape off an ink jet cartridge prior to placing in the printer.
46. When going to a store to purchase replacement ink jet or toner cartridges, either take the empty cartridge or write down the cartridge number (Not the printer make and model).
47. Do not share any Windows or other passwords.
48. Treat an external hard drive like a flash drive.
49. Plug items like mice, keyboard and speaker around back to free up front USB ports.
50. When having a problem, power off everything and then turn everything back on.

Follow these tips to make your computing life easier.

44. QUESTIONS AND ANSWERS

Should I turn off my computer or leave it on at the end of the day?

Unless the computer needs to remain on for any reason, properly shut it down when finished. In my opinion, the benefits of saving power, keeping the computer cooler and clearing out the RAM outweigh the possibility of possibly wearing out the hard drive sooner.

How do I check my system specifications?

The system specifications including the processor speed, Windows version on the system and memory can be checked under CONTROL PANEL / SYSTEM.

My Computer doesn't seem to keep the correct date and time.

The computer's CMOS battery is failing and may need to be replaced. The computer can be used with a failing CMOS battery as long as the correct date and time is entered each time the computer is turned on.

How can I update the device drivers on my computer?

Select CONTROL PANEL / DEVICE MANAGER. Each system device will be listed. Right Click on each system device and select UPDATE. Windows will automatically check for updated drivers for each device.

I am a long time AOL user. What is happening with them?

AOL was purchased by Verizon and I still don't understand why. AOL users can still use their AOL accounts at the time of this writing.

Why won't Windows Update?

- Check the date and time on the computer. If the date or time is incorrect, Windows won't update.
- Make sure that the computer is online.
- Is a firewall blocking the updates?
- Check the system rights. A non-administrator user account may not be permitted to run updates.
- Check for viruses. Run a full scan of the computer and verify there isn't a virus or Trojan that is causing Windows Updates to fail.

Can I move an old hard drive into a different computer and just reactivate Windows with the replacement computer?

Probably not. When Windows is activated online, it references the key code with the specific hardware – motherboard, video, etc. Unless you are removing the hard drive and placing it in the exact computer, it may not activate. If the original hard drive fails, it can be replaced with a new hard drive and Windows will automatically activate once online.

I just had a virus removed from my computer. My account works fine, but a different account on the computer still can't get on the Internet. Why?

Viruses removed under a single account don't mean that viruses were removed under all user accounts. Certain viruses and hijackers may affect a single user account only, but not the others. All accounts should be checked for viruses, not just the main user account.

What's really the best Anti-Virus Program?

Remember that no single program removes every problem file and program and things change quickly in the computer market. What I list may not be recommended 3-6 months from now. For pay programs, I like Norton. The best freeware programs are Windows Defender, Superantispyware Free and Malwarebytes Free Edition.

I cannot open photo attachments that were emailed.

Double click on the photo and Windows responds with a list of potential programs to open the photo because Windows can't find a program to open the attachment.

Select one of the programs, use one of the Windows recommended programs, the PAINT program or download ADOBE READER from Adobe's website. If the files don't open, the computer could be virused

The Computer is noisy.

Computer noise can be caused by the power supply, noisy CPU or video fan or hard drive (which is not a good noise). Take these steps to quiet a noisy computer:

1. Shoot compressed air into the power supply to see if that quiets it down.
2. Next open the side panel of a desktop to find out where the noise is originating.
3. Sometime a loose cable can be striking a fan. Move and secure all cables away from any spinning fans.
4. A clicking noise from the hard drive probably means the drive will fail soon. If the noise is originating from the hard drive, BACKUP YOUR IMPORTANT FILES ASAP.

I was re-installing Windows and power is lost during the process. Will it be OK if I pick up the process from where it shut down?

Turn it on and let the process continue uninterrupted. If the process continues without a single error message, the reload process MAY have corrected itself. Restart the entire process from the beginning if any error messages appear about files not being copied correctly.

Why does Windows sometimes restart without my direction to restart?

If the computer is set to AUTO UPDATE, Windows will automatically download and install updates. Windows needs to restart after updates. To turn off automatic updates, Select WINDOWS UPDATE / CHANGE SETTINGS / DOWNLOAD UPDATES BUT LET ME CHOOSE WHETHER TO INSTALL THEM.

Why won't Windows let me delete a certain file or folder?

Windows will not allow a user to delete any file or folder currently in use. Restart the computer and attempt to again delete the file. The file may be an integral part of Windows or the user may not have administrator privileges to delete the file in question.

I cannot find a program to open a file on a computer.

Select the program and attempt to open the file through the program. If the file will not open, Windows can automatically search the Internet in an attempt to find a program to open the file. If the file still doesn't open, read the error message and write down the file extension and search for a solution online.

Why did a new web browser toolbar appear on my browser? Is it safe and how can I remove it?

Most "free" downloads install extra unwanted programs on a computer like extra toolbars. Run Malwarebytes and Superantispyware to remove any unwanted spyware from the computer. The unwanted toolbars should remove using the Install Program under Control Panel / Programs / Remove Programs.

I want to use Apache Open Office or other program instead of Microsoft Office because it's free. Are there any limitations?

Apache Open Office is adequate for letter writing, spreadsheets. Keep in mind that a switch should be set in Apache Open Office that will make the program automatically open and close as Microsoft Office documents, so the program will be compatible with any MS Office files.

To setup the program to always open and close as a Microsoft document: Open the Text or Spreadsheet program within Apache Open Office and then Select TOOLS / OPTIONS / LOAD and SAVE / GENERAL and the under the ALWAYS SAVE AS option / Select MS WORD 97/2000/XP option.

Does it matter if external devices are not removed safely?

Yes. Removing a flash drive while in use can damage the drive and lose data. Click on the SAFELY REMOVE HARDWARE icon on the Taskbar and wait for the prompt that states IT IS NOW SAFE TO REMOVE THE HARDWARE.

Why do I have to accept Windows updates?

Most of the Windows updates are security related so accept them, unless the computer is never on the Internet.

I'm having a problem with the computer manufacturer that I feel they should address, but I cannot get any response. Is there anything I can do?

If the manufacturer doesn't respond or responds and the answer isn't to your satisfaction, file a complaint with the online BBB. Manufacturers don't like online complaints.

How does a computer connect to a TV?

Hulu, Netflix, Amazon and other subscription streaming services are the trend to interact streaming downloads and the Internet with a TV. Netflix and Hulu feature previously viewed movies and TV shows. Required are high speed Internet access and a computer capable of handling the feed. It's best to use a desktop with a separate video card and cabled high speed Internet (not wireless).

A television can accept multiple input feeds. The cable can be directly connected to the TV through the cable input though a computer HDMI or VGA video cable feed. To switch TV output from the cable feed to the computer, use the INPUT control on the television remote. Newer televisions are now Internet capable but have limited web browsing capability.

Why can't I send out a particular file attachment through e-mail?

The file may be too large. Either break up the file to send smaller parts, convert the file to PDF or find a site that will permit downloads of larger files to send the file from.

I'm purchasing a new computer. Should I consider a computer with an Intel or AMD processor and does it make any difference?

In general AMD processors run hotter than Intel processors because they "overclock" their processors. They cannot sell their processors at the same price as Intel because of the perceived quality difference. It depends on what the computer is being used for. Do your homework on the computer itself prior to making a purchase.

Questions and Answers to most problems can be found online.

45. THE BEST FREE STUFF

If it's free it's for me. As discussed earlier, the Internet is loaded with free downloads, programs, coupons or anything the marketing geniuses can come up with to get a user's attention to visit their website. Free stuff is great. If the program doesn't work out, uninstall it and look for the next great free thing. It's the best feeling in the world when you find a free program that works and is actually useful.

THE PRICE OF "FREE"

Nothing online is really free. Personal information is exchanged for something the user perceives of value. In many cases the user agrees to accept solicitation emails from the company and their affiliates. It's a small price to pay in exchange to get a program that can possibly help a computing experience.

TRIAL SOFTWARE

Many software companies will give a full version trial or evaluation copy of their software. The software will work for 30 days and then shut down. The software companies are betting that once a user tries their software and invests time on learning how to use it that the user will shell out the money to purchase.

ADVERTISER PAID SOFTWARE

Companies will provide free software online. A downloader must view or click through other advertiser ads and links prior to downloading the free program or utility. The free program download is being subsidized by the ads, which is why the program can be offered free.

FREEWARE / SHAREWARE

This type of software is truly free. The developer may ask for donations, but it won't shut down after a trial period. Review the program of interest prior to downloading. Remember that many of these programs probably offer a pay version upgrade. Use the free program first to see if it's worth the money to upgrade to the pay version.

NINITE

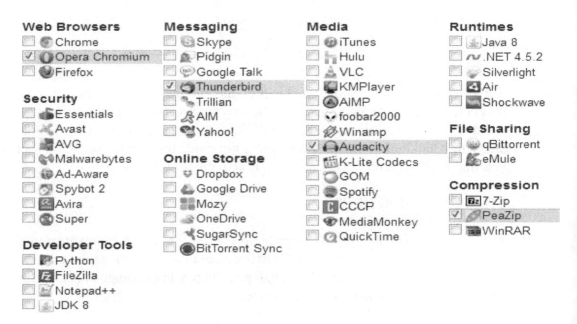

This is a screen shot from a website called NINITE. Ninite.com is a great website to find all kinds of free software. Programs are categorized under the type of functionality it serves. We use Ninite to download multiple programs for system preps.

FAVORITES

Our favorite free programs are listed below:

1. Anti-virus   Microsoft Defender
2. Spyware Removal   Superantispyware Free Edition
3. Malware Removal   Malware Bytes Free Edition
4. Browser Cleanup   Manually clean the browser
5. System Cleanup   RKill 64, Junkware Removal Tool
6. Word Processing   Apache Open Office / Google Docs online
7. System Optimization   Glary Utilites, CCleaner
8. Hard Disk Defragmenter   Defraggler
9. Online Storage   One Drive, Dropbox (limited space)
10. Media / Movie Player   VLC Media Player
11. Music Player – online   Spotify & Slacker
12. Email   Google Gmail
13. PDF Reader   Adobe Reader
14. Free item search   Craigslist.com
15. Free data storage (limited)   Dropbox
16. Free shareware programs   CNET or download.com

BE CAREFUL OF FREE STUFF

Remember our earlier discussions on "Free" stuff. Research any "free" program prior to downloading and testing.

FREE REPAIR HELP WEBSITES

Listed below are the three best free computer help sites for software and advice.

1. Bleepingcomputer.com
2. Ifixit.com
3. Tomshardware.com
4. Secondsourcecomputers.com – free computer tech tips only.

This free stuff may prove useful.

46. SMART PHONES

SMART PHONES

Who doesn't have a smart phone? Smart phones are integral part of life for many individuals, but it's important to be aware of potential problems that may arise from their use.

COMMON SMART PHONE PROBLEMS

Smart phones can be easily damaged by improper handling and storage. Don't expose a phone to water or use wet hands to push the buttons. Exposing a phone to prolonged excessive heat can damage the battery or internal components. Leaving the smart phone in extremely cold temperatures could possibly cause a temporary loss of the screen display as well as battery damage.

CHARGING / POWER PROBLEMS

1. If a phone doesn't turn on, see if the battery is fully charged.
2. Connect the phone to its charger. Plug the charger in, wait for a few seconds, and then turn the phone on.
3. Turn off the phone, take out the battery, replace the battery and turn the phone on again. Attempt to charge again.
4. Use a different battery and charger of the same type; use them to work out if the issue is with the phone, the battery, or the charger.

DROPPED or BREAKING CALLS

Dropped calls or low sound quality during calls can be caused by low signal strength or temporary gaps in network coverage. Move the phone to a different place to increase its signal strength. If inside a building, move towards a window. Contact the network provider first for help with signal strength issues.

PHONE ACTS WACKY

For any unusual problem, switch the phone off, and remove the SIM card. Re-power the phone on again without the SIM card in it. Turn off the phone, replace the SIM and call again. If this doesn't work, use a different SIM card in the phone to work out whether the problem is with the handset or the SIM chip.

CLONING

A phone is cloned when someone steals its unique electronic serial number and telephone number. This allows the thief to charge unauthorized calls to the account. If you believe to be a victim of cloning, contact your cellular phone carrier immediately.

IPHONES

The Apple IPhone is a very popular Internet- and multimedia-enabled smartphone with over 400,000 applications approved by Apple. The iPhone is the standard by which other phones and applications are measured.

COMMON IPHONE PROBLEMS

IPhones can have problems.

IPHONE SLOWS OR FREEZES

When an iPhone freezes, it's probably related to issues with specific mobile apps. To correct the freeze itself, force the iPhone to shut down by holding down the power button and the home button simultaneously. The iPhone should shut down after 10 seconds. The problem may be corrected after restarting the phone.

If freezing or slowness becomes a recurring issue, experiment with uninstalling each installed applications and re-installing them one at a time. When phone begins freezing again, the problem app has been found.

CRACKED SCREEN

A cracked screen is the most common phone problem. IPhone screens are typically easy to replace than Samsung Galaxy phones. Review a YouTube a video on the repair prior to attempting. Assume a cost of $100-$150 to have a repair shop do the repair.

BROKEN POWER JACK

A broken power jack is a repair for a skilled technician. Review videos on the repair prior to attempting.

DROPPED CALLS

IPhone may drop a call in the middle of a conversation even in an area with full bars, or iPhone signal may change drastically without moving the physical location of the phone. There isn't much one can do about dropped calls with the iPhone, other than contacting the wireless carrier. See if the iPhone is upgraded to the latest version of the operating system, and if the phone is still dropping calls, schedule an appointment with an Apple Genius at the Apple store; however, this is a known issue, and there's probably nothing Apple can do to address this particular problem.

IPHONE FACTORY RESET

Factory resetting an IPhone can fix most fixes can be effective for resolving IPhone issues.

1. Use the lock button to turn the screen off and on again.
2. Hold down the Sleep/Wake and Home buttons until the Apple logo appears to reset your iPhone.
3. Perform a factory reset on the phone.

FIXING A DISABLED IPHONE

Here's how to put an iPhone into Recovery Mode:

1. Plug the USB cable into a computer but do not connect it to the iPhone.
2. Launch iTunes.
3. Press and hold down the Home button and Sleep/Wake button for 10 seconds until the iPhone powers off.
4. Keep hold of the Home button but let go of the Sleep/Wake button.

TOUCH SCREEN DOESN'T WORK

Make sure that your hands are clean and dry, then follow these steps:

1. Remove any screen protector on the device.
2. Clean the screen with a soft, slightly damp, lint-free cloth.
3. Unplug the device.
4. Restart the device. If the device doesn't restart, force a restart by powering off and back on.

SECURE A SMART PHONE

Phones are becoming more secure with fingerprint and facial recognition. If you do not want to go to those security extremes, these older methods are still effective.

1. **USE A PIN CODE**

   Use a 4-digit numeric pass code to keep unauthorized users from using your phone and it's not that much of an inconvenience.

2. **HAVE A STRONG PASSWORD ONLINE**

   Have a password that mixes letters, numbers, upper and lower case.

3. **KNOW WHAT IS BEING DOWNLOADED**

   Remember that phones can get viruses. Be careful on what is being downloaded to any phone just like a computer.

ANDROID PHONES

With any android phone problem, Reset the phone back to factory settings. If your data is saved off the phone into the cloud, this should not be an issue. If the factory reset does not solve the problem, the phone hardware needs to be examined.

Follow the same advice given earlier on broken glass and jack repairs.

COMMON ANDROID PROBLEMS

1. **CANNOT LOGIN INTO MANUFACTURER ACCOUNT AFTER FACTORY RESET.**

   May be a problem with the Phone OS installed. Back grade or upgrade OS. Contact the service provider or manufacturer.

2. **BATTERY DRAINS QUICKLY**

   Lower the BRIGHTNESS and EXTEND BATTERY in SETTINGS.

3. **PHONE SLOWS UP OR FREEZES**

   Look to free up space on the phone and remove unused Apps.

4. **CONNECTION ISSUES**

   Enable AIRPLANE MODE for 30 seconds and then turn it off.

5. **STALLED TEXT MESSAGE**

   Select RESEND to check that text went through

Smart phones can act up. Learn to reset a phone and back up important data.

47. GAMING, TABLET, TV REPAIRS AND INTERNET SERVICE PROVIDERS

Computers and phones aren't the only electronic equipment that needs repairing. As a bonus, here's a list of non-computer electronic products that break and a quick whether to repair or not.

GAMING CONSOLES

XBOX, WII, PS4 and older game stations may have encountered the "red ring" problem. The ring problem is caused by the unit CPU overheating. An XBOX has a better chance of being repaired if more rings display. The CPU needs to be re-seated along with a new coating of thermal paste and the board has to be reflowed.

If the unit displays one ring or an error code 74, get the unit repaired or replaced by the manufacturer. If a drive isn't reading, the laser or optical drive probably should be replaced. It's rare that a drive cleaning will correct that type of problem. Check the unit with multiple game CDs to verify that the problem is with the unit and not a game CD. Any onboard video problems are not worth fixing – send the unit to the manufacturer for repair or replace it.

Video problems can be caused because the console isn't properly setup with a TV or something was changed. Shut off the gaming unit and TV and re-power everything back up. HDMI Port repairs are not worth paying for; the repair won't hold up.

The repair may be worth it if the cost is $100 or less. When the unit is back from repair, reset the unit because it may have been tested on a different type of television.

If the gaming unit is sent back to Sony or Microsoft, the usual repair cost is approximately $150. All information on the hard drive will be lost. When units are shipped to the manufacturer for repair, the units are replaced.

TABLETS / iPADS

Android Tablets and IPods can experience these types of problems:

1. GENERAL SOFTWARE OR INTERNET PROBLEMS

The easiest way to correct any software issue with a tablet is to RESET it. Check under SYSTEM or SETTINGS and find RESET TO FACTORY. Assuming data is backed up, resetting back to factory defaults should not be an issue.

2. CRACKED SCREEN

A cracked screen gets replaced, not repaired. Assume a repair cost of at least $100 to $150. Determine whether it's better value to simply replace the unit.

3. BROKEN AC POWER JACK

Assume a repair cost of at least $100-$150 to replace an AC power jack. Determine whether a broken jack is worth the repair cost versus replacing the unit.

LCD TVs

There is a reason that television repair shops are hard to find. Televisions are so inexpensive that in most cases, it won't make sense to repair a broken television.

Size matters when determining whether to repair a television or not. Any television below a 40-50in size should just be recycled and replaced. It's hard to take larger televisions to the repair shop.

It may make sense to purchase extended warranties on larger TVs, if the warranty includes in-home service. Contact the TV manufacturer online to locate the closest repair facility.

CAMERAS

The most common problem with cameras is a failed memory card. Copy camera photos directly to a PC or online for backup. Cameras are another electronic disposable item. Assuming the camera is not under warranty, weigh the cost of the repair versus replacement. Check online with the camera manufacturer to get an estimate. Most camera and electronic store send the camera out for repair anyway.

FIOS / CABLE REPAIRS

Cable repairs is mostly powering off and restarting either the individual box or the entire setup in the basement. Is the problem with a single set or every set in the home?

PROBLEM WITH A SINGLE TV

First check the input selection – make sure the TV isn't set to DVD or different input device. Assuming the problem is at one TV, pull the power to the box to reset that individual box and reconnect and power up. That should repair the problem.

If resetting the box doesn't correct the problem, change box locations. Move the problem box on a different TV to confirm if the problem is with the converter box only.

WHOLE HOUSE PROBLEM

With FIOS or cable, when the entire house loses TV, head to the basement (or wherever they installed the main console) and check the power plug from the console to the outlet. Most likely the breaker for that console is thrown. Reset the breaker. If that doesn't correct the problem, call the company.

Follow these guidelines on dealing with non-computer repairs.

48. DIAGNOSE MOST PROBLEMS IN 5 MINUTES

Use this checklist to become the Speedy Gonzales Computer Repair person in your neighborhood.

1. **FIRST THINGS FIRST**

   Turn off power and attempt to repower everything. This includes the modem and wireless router if the problem is Internet related.

2. **NOTEBOOK HARDWARE PROBLEM QUICK CHECKS**

   - Remove the notebook battery and attempt to power the note book up with AC charger only.
   - Use a replacement AC charger.
   - If the notebook jack needs to be moved to turn on the notebook, the jack needs to be soldered or replaced ($150).
   - If a notebook display shows no video; however, video appears on an external monitor when connected to the notebook, the problem is with an Inverter or LCD screen ($100-250).
   - If the problem is no power and no image on the LCD AND external monitor, most likely the motherboard in the notebook has failed and it's not worth repairing.

3. RUN SYSTEM HARDWARE TESTS

The computer system BIOS hardware tests are a good quick way to check for any hardware failure.

- Get into the SETUP utility when turning on the computer (F1, F2, or DELETE Key).
- Check under the menus for DIAGNOSTICS or HARDWARE TESTS.
- Hardware diagnostics should check the memory and hard drive.

4. COMPUTER TURNS ON BUT DOESN'T START WINDOWS

- Windows should automatically attempt to repair itself.
- If the computer doesn't start in SAFE MODE, attempt to run a Windows REPAIR.
- Run a CHKDISK REPAIR. Download a bootable hard disk repair program. Check for a freeware program at CNET.
- Re-install Windows. Data will be lost. To save data, the hard drive needs to be pulled and data transferred to another computer for saving. If the computer starts in SAFE MODE, the problem may possibly be corrected without a Windows re-installation.

5. USE THE PRINCIPLE OF HALVES

Whenever possible use the Principle of Halves to diagnose any problem. Swap or test with a different part whenever possible. Some examples:

- Swap a monitor or plug in a test external monitor on a notebook to test a video problem.
- Move a printer to a different computer or attempt a printer print test.
- With a notebook keyboard problem, plug in an external USB keyboard.

Use the Principle of Halves to help diagnose computer problems. Power off everything and restart to begin diagnosing.

APPENDIX

a) Know this screen

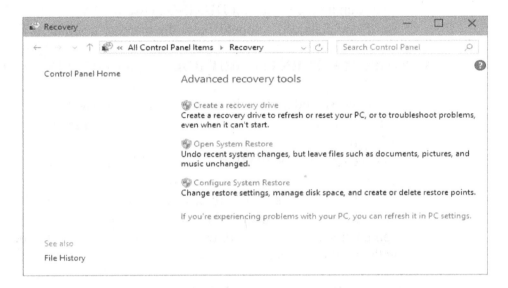

Learn the RECOVERY screen and how to use the features in it to correct most Windows problems. This may be the most important Windows screen to learn.

TO ACCESS THIS SCREEN

To access this screen, Select CONTROL PANEL / RECOVERY

RESTORE POINT

A restore point is a snapshot of Windows settings at a certain point in time. Creating a restore point will allow the user to recover the Windows settings back to that point in time when Windows was working properly.

Restore points are listed chronologically from the most recent restore point at the top of the list to the oldest restore point at the bottom. It is best to attempt recovering using the most recent restore point first.

TO CREATE A RESTORE POINT

- Select CONFIGURE SYSTEM RESTORE
- Select the C Drive and make sure that PROTECTION IS ON
- Select CREATE and NAME THE BACKUP

TO RECOVER USING A RESTORE POINT

- Select CONTROL PANEL / RECOVERY
- Select OPEN SYSTEM RESTORE
- Find a restore point to recover from and select it. The process may take up to ½ hour.

The Restore Point is the less invasive recovery option because it should not affect any programs or files. If the Restore point does not work, the next step is to RESET THE COMPUTER.

The RESET feature is located on the same page, below the Restore Point options. A RESET can be run either saving files or not saving files, however PROGRAMS WILL BE LOST AND HAVE TO BE RE-INSTALLED. Microsoft Office will have to be re-installed, even if the SAVE FILES OPTION is selected.

TO RESET A COMPUTER

- Select CONTROL PANEL / RECOVERY or PC SETTINGS / SECURITY & UPDATES / RECOVERY
- Choose the option that states "If you are experiencing problems with your PC, you can refresh it in PC Settings".
- Select the RESET either SAVING FILES or NOT SAVING FILES. The process will take hours.
- After the RESET completes, check for Windows updates and re-install programs.

Learn to make and recover using Restore Points and how to RESET a Windows PC.

b) Apple, Windows, Android, Phones

Fifteen years ago choices were simple. Use either a PC or Apple computer to access the internet and a cell phone to text. Today users have options like netbooks, tablets, iPads, android phones, iPhones, smart TVs and wrist watches.

REASONS FOR VARIOUS DEVICES

The primary reason for computers and devices is Internet access, which includes entertainment, news, weather and other work related activities. The secondary reason would be for business – financial, word processing, spreadsheets, and other activities.

WHAT'S BEST TO USE?

It depends on the person and activity. I prefer a traditional computer or laptop because of the larger screen and keyboard size. Most seniors probably feel the same way.

Younger people are raised using their phones for most everything – communication, entertainment, gaming, news and pretty much everything. I still can't see typing a term paper on a phone, but maybe that's just me.

WINDOWS VERSUS APPLE

I've used both PCs and Apple equipment and prefer Windows-based systems mainly for the abundance of free applications available. I also prefer to be in the camp with 75% of all users instead of the other 25%. Apple equipment is more expensive to fix out of warranty, Macs do get virused and software is more expensive.

HOW TO HANDLE APPLE REPAIRS

Most Apple systems can have their operating system (OSX) re-installed by pressing the <COMMAND> Key Plus "R" key on system startup. The user should be directed to their Repair menu which allows a user to do one of the following:

- Re-Install the OSX operating system.
- Restore from a time machine backup.
- Access the hard drive to repair the drive.

Other useful Apple commands are the <COMMAND> key plus the "S" key, which will allow the Apple system to be set back to factory by keying in some commands. If you unsure how to proceed, Google how to reinstall OSX with your particular Apple System. Pressing the <OPTION> key on startup will allow the user to start the Apple system from a bootable device such as a USB or DVD with OSX installed.

Apple systems typically require a set of "star" shaped screwdrivers to remove the screws from Apple systems or notebooks. A set of screwdrivers can be purchased on EBay or Amazon for $15-20.

ANDROID TABLETS VERSUS IPad TABLETS

The Apple IPad is a superior product to lower end Android tablets. Either can be repaired for any software problem by RESETTING the unit. Most tablet resets are performed under the SYSTEM or SETTINGS options. Learn to reset either an IPad or Android tablet.

IPHONES VERSUS ANDROID PHONES

I am definitely an iPhone supporter, however like older people go kicking and screaming every time I have to upgrade my phone.

INTERNET SERVICE

In my area the two main choices are Comcast or Verizon. Both have their advantages and disadvantages. Make sure to know when your contract expires and call at least 60 days ahead of time to negotiate your best deal.

Understand how you plan to use an Internet device before purchasing.

c) Other Useful Stuff

This chapter was added after we completed the glossary. If this information seems disjointed, attribute that feeling to our laziness to redo everything. We aren't expecting this book to win any Pulitzer prizes anyway.

COPY FILES TO A FLASH DRIVE

1. Navigate to the folder that contains the files to copy.

2. Plug the USB flash drive into a USB port on the computer.

3. Make sure the USB drive has enough free space to copy the files. Find a place on the USB drive to store the copied files.

4. Drag the file(s) from the computer to the USB drive OR you can also right click on the folder to copy and Select SEND TO and select the USB drive (Usually D, E, F, G or lower letter).

5. Eject the drive safely using the flash drive icon on the bottom right of the taskbar.

MAKE A SHORTCUT ON THE DESKTOP USING WINDOWS 10

1. Select the APPS option.

2. Right-click on the app to create a desktop shortcut

3. Select the CREATE SHORTCUT option.

TURN OFF SLEEP MODE

Sleep mode can cause more problems than it solves. Computers may not recover from sleep mode or take so long to wake up that users believe the computer is not working properly and the computer. To turn off sleep mode:

1. Select CONTROL PANEL and POWER OPTIONS.

2. Select CHANGE PLAN SETTINGS.

3. Under PUT COMPUTER TO SLEEP, Select NEVER.

DVD STUCK IN A DVD DRIVE

To remove a DVD from a DVD drive that will not open:

1. First attempt to eject the DVD though Windows: Select MY PC / Right Click on the DVD icon and select EJECT.

2. If the DVD drive will not open straighten a paper clip.

3. The DVD drive has a small hole on the front face panel. This hole is placed on the DVD as an emergency eject in case the DVD drive breaks.

4. Force the now straight paper clip into the hole until the DVD drive begins to open. Once the DVD is slightly ejected, use your fingers to fully open the DVD drive.

INSTALLING A PROGRAM

When installing a program follow the following rules:

1. If the program to install was downloaded to the computer, the installation file can usually be found in the folder titled DOWNLOADS, unless the download was directed to a different location.

2. If installing printer software, DO NOT physically connect the printer to the computer until the installation program instructs you to.

3. Select the default option chosen by the installation program unless you know to select a different option.

WEBCAM SOFTWARE

Windows 10 includes Webcam software that works with most webcams. Select APPS and then CAMERA to access the webcam on your computer.

CHANGE TIME ZONE

If the time zone is incorrect on the computer:

1. Select the RUN COMMAND

2. Type CHANGE TIME ZONE and <ENTER>.

3. Click on the link that says CHANGE THE TIME ZONE.

4. Select the correct time zone and OK.

VIDEO OUTPUTS

Notebooks and laptops have video outputs that allow the connection of an external monitor to the laptop for display purposes. Video inputs can be handy for testing of a video problem. Types of video outputs include:

VGA

The VGA port is the oldest video port connection and will be found on older laptops and notebooks.

DVI

DVI came after VGA, however many laptops and notebooks used the VGA output port, since the technology was already developed and less expensive to use.

HDMI

HDMI is the newest video output and found on most laptops, notebooks and televisions. Many people will connect a portable device to a large television for a better viewing experience.

NOTE: To switch the view from the device screen to the external monitor, either the SOURCE has to be changed on the monitor to VGA, DVI or HDMI or the source has to be changed using the TV remote to the proper viewing option.

FILE FORMATS

A file format is how the data within the file is organized. A program t must be able to recognize and possibly access data within the file. For example, a Web browser can process and display files in HTML format but it cannot display a file in a format designed for Microsoft Word. .

FILE EXTENSION

A file extension is separated by a period from the name and contains three or four letters that identify the format. The most popular Identification method is to determine the format of a file based on the end of its name—the letters following the final period. For example, website HTML documents are identified by names that end with .html (or .htm).

There are as many different file formats as there are different programs to process the files. A few of the more common file formats are:

Word documents (.doc)

Web text pages (.htm or .html)

Web page images (.gif and .jpg)

Adobe Postscript files (.ps)

Adobe Acrobat files (.pdf)

Executable programs (.exe)

Multimedia and video files (.mp3, mp4 and others)

PDF FILES

One of the most commonly used file formats is PDF. PDF files are used to send larger files because PDF files are send compressed and take up less space are quicker to send.

PDF READER

Newer versions of Microsoft Word can save and convert Word Documents to PDF files. If you don't have Microsoft Word, download the free version of Adobe PDF reader from the adobe website for reading PDF files.

One can never have too much useful information where computers are concerned.

d) Free Computer Help & hiring me

You can get free computer help at secondsourcecomputers.com. Weekly blog posts are published or you can sign up for our free tech tips newsletter. You can also get discounted product pricing on notebooks and printer ink and toner from that website.

If you would like my assistance on any computer issue I can be reached at pcwhispereronline@gmail.com. I charge $29.99 per single occurrence or $99.99 for a year's personal computer retainer service.

Besides extensive home user and small business repair background, I also have extensive business experience with expertise in Point of Sale, Retail, Inventory control, system selection and implementation, cost justification issues with system integration and on-going support. Initial business contact is free. Email to pcwhispereronline@gmail.com.

Place in the subject line "I READ YOUR BOOK" and include a brief background of the computer system and problem, along with the make and model of the computer. I'll determine whether I can help you and respond to your email. If you want anything from the secondsourcecomputers.com website, also place the notation "I READ YOUR BOOK" to get an additional 10% -20% off the listed product price.

Payment can be made by PayPal or credit card. In the case of a credit card payment, we will call and take the credit card number over the phone so your number is not compromised over the internet.

I can help you determine how to correct your problem, retrieve your data or determine whether your computer problem is worth investing money for a repair. I also drop ship warranted refurbished notebook and discounted printer ink and toner. We are also a long time EBay Power Seller and can also provide online buying and selling advice using EBay, Amazon or PayPal.

Just in case you require help.

e) About SECOND SOURCE COMPUTERS

SECOND SOURCE: MORE THAN JUST USED COMPUTERS

Conveniently located at Marsh and Silverside Roads in North Wilmington, Second Source was recognized by *The News Journal* readers as the "Best in Delaware for computer repair."

Second Source Computer Center has gained an outstanding reputation by buying, selling and trading new and used computers for more than 14 years. The range of services and products Second Source provides makes it a one-stop shopping option for new and experienced computer customers. According to Ken Jaskulski, "In a sense we're a victim our own success." Because Second Source is now

> ### Second Source Computer Center
> **Marsh & Silverside Rds.**
> **Wilmington, DE**
> **(302) 475-7018**

so well-known for buying, selling and trading new and used computers, many customers are not aware of the company's other services.

NEW SYSTEMS. For more than 14 years Second Source has been selling reliable custom-built Amtech products. Customers appreciate the easy upgradability and servicability of these top-of-the-line systems. Amtech PCs come with an excellent in-store continued on page 2

SECOND SOURCE

(cont. from page 1)

warranty. These machines are dependable, reliable, easy to repair and can be easily upgraded. Ask about the many features of the P 1.5 GHz PC ($999 new) or the 750 MGHz PC ($599 new). One big advantage of buying an Amtech is the burn-in, or testing, that Second Source performs on all of its new units. All Amtechs receive a high level of testing prior to customer pickup in order to make sure that the PC is working properly. Second Source exceeds the testing level that major PC manufacturers such as Dell and Gateway employ.

Let the staff of Second Source handle all your computer needs. Hardware, software, service, special orders and consultations.

"Over eighty-five percent of computer problems are not hardware related," Jaskulski said. If a virus, an accidental deletion or a program conflict has made the PC inoperable, Second Source has a solution. For a worse case scenario, an optional system recovery disk is available on the Amtech PCs that will reset the entire unit. With purchase of a new or used computer, free in-store training is offered.

TRAINING. Second Source is committed to providing education and information to its customers. From in-store training classes to on-site training, the experts at Second Source work with customers to find the right program for individuals and businesses. It's recommended that on-site training customers generate a list of issues and questions prior to the session to tailor it specifically to their needs. This personalized approach is the hallmark of Second Source.

SERVICE. Jaskulski is proud of the recognition readers of *The News Journal* gave Second Source by voting it as the "Best in Delaware for Computer Repair" for 2001. "It's a testament to the benefits of a small, independent store versus the super store," Jaskulski said. Second Source builds personal relationships with its customers with knowledgeable, friendly service. At a smaller store, purchasing a PC is akin to buying a car from a full-service dealer, while super stores treat it like the purchase of an appliance. At Second Source the average service time is just three to seven days from check-in to the workbench, but expedited service options are available. On-site and dial-in or remote diagnostic service is also available for an additional cost.

LASER PRINTER & MONITOR REPAIR. Finding a reliable, local company that repairs laser printers and monitors is now as easy as stopping by Second Source. The team of technicians is able to fix a wide range of printers and monitors. You'll be told prior to checking in the item if it's worth fixing.

NETWORKS. Second Source installs small to medium size networks in homes or businesses.

INTERNET SERVICES Second Source is a complete Internet Service Provider (ISP) with phone dial-up and high-speed Comcast cable access. A new Web site, superlocaldeals.com (being developed) will give local businesses a forum to advertise exclusive discounts and will provide customers with a great place to save. Customers will be able to print out coupons and take them to the stores for savings. "The idea behind the Web site is to use the Internet to help people shop locally, instead of mail order," Jaskulski said.

RECYCLING. "We have partnered with a local recycling company," Jaskulski said. "Anything that we don't buy, we refer to our recycling partner, select nonprofits or the Delaware Solid Waste Authority. The last thing we want is people dumping their computers in the trash and filling our landfills with this stuff."

CONSULTATION. "I take pride in the fact that I am now the least knowledgeable computer person at the store," said Jaskulski. He has 20 years of experience in computers and has created training videos, but Jaskulski believes his staff is more in tune with the cutting edge technology. The staff is truly exceptional and they are equally adept at working with brand new users and the true techies. "The people we hire must love working with computers. Even our part-timers are Microsoft-certified and have been doing computer consulting for many years." An example of the consultation work that Second Source provides is the advice they offer regarding application-specific software (example: buying software to run a restaurant or insurance company). According to Jaskulski, "This software can expose customers to problems down the road if the proper steps are not employed to protect them. We take a top-to-bottom approach to consulting."

SPECIAL ORDERS. Second Source works with customers to special order any product that they need. The staff researches and finds the right parts and the best prices. "I almost forgot. We still buy, sell and trade new and used computers," Jaskulski said.

Whether you are buying a new system, having a service problem or selling equipment, Second Source is a must-stop for all of your computer needs. *Open seven days a week. Visa, Mastercard, Discover, American Express and personal checks accepted. Financing is available. Call (302) 475-7018 for more information.*

f) Quick Reference Guide

COMPUTER RUNS SLOW

a) Check the system specifications.
b) Too many programs loading on Startup. Run MSCONFIG and turn off programs in STARTUP and non-Microsoft programs under SERVICES.
c) Scan the hard drive to check for bad sectors using Ultimate or Active boot disk. Check the hard drive health.
d) Scan the computer for viruses or spyware
e) Run DISK CLEANUP and DISK DEFRAGMENTER.
f) Re-install Windows and format the hard drive during the process.

CANNOT ACCESS THE INTERNET

IF THE PROBLEM IS BOTH WIRED AND WIRELESS.

a) Use a different browser or Reset the web browser settings.
b) Reset the modem by removing power plug.
c) If using BOTH a modem and router, remove plug to turn off the power to both devices.
d) Restart the computer and test the Internet in SAFE MODE WITH NETWORKING.
e) Check for viruses, spyware and malware.
f) A firewall may be preventing Internet access. Turn off any security suites.
f) Access Internet on a different computer to determine if the problem is with the Internet provider.

WIRELESS ONLY PROBLEM

a) Is the wireless device turned on?
b) Does the notebook see any wireless connections? If other wireless networks are available and yours is not, there may be a problem with the network.
c) Right click on the wireless icon on the bottom right of the Taskbar and run REPAIR.
d) If the Repair doesn't work, power off, re-power the computer and restart.
e) Repower the modem and wireless router (if being used) and computer and try again. Restart the modem first and the computer last.
f) Take a notebook elsewhere and attempt to access a different wireless network or try a different wireless computer on the network to isolate the problem.
g) Check Device Manager to see if there are any bad, missing or disabled wireless network drivers.
h) Attempt to connect in SAFE MODE WITH NETWORKING.

COMPUTER DOESN'T START WINDOWS

a) Re-start the computer by powering it off and back on.
b) Check that a bootable external device isn't causing the problem – remove any DVD or flash drive from the system.
c) Restart the computer in SAFE MODE (Press F8 on startup or restart holding down WINDOWS Key). If Windows starts in SAFE MODE, the problem is software related – virus, spyware or device driver issue that may be fixable without re-installing Windows.
d) Restart the computer in with Windows Repair Flash or USB Drive. Run Repair options
d) If SAFE MODE works, check the video settings under DISPLAY. Change the RESOLUTION to a minimum 1024 by 768 resolution and restart the computer.
e) If the problem happened immediately after a WINDOWS UPDATE or DEVICE DRIVER UPDATE, attempt to ROLL BACK the driver in Device Manager.
f) Run a CHKDSK or SCANDISK repair from a bootable CD or flash drive like Ultimate Boot Disk, Hirens, Active Boot Disk or another bootable program.
g) Either RESET or RE-INSTALL Windows.

NO SOUND

a) Check that the speaker connector cable is plugged into correct spot, speakers have power, are turned on and volume control knob is turned up at least half way.
b) Check that the sound isn't MUTED or volume set to a very low setting.
c) Move the speakers on a different computer.
d) Check Device Manager and be sure there aren't any sound device driver conflicts.

NO VIDEO

a) Check that the computer is not in HIBERNATION or POWER SAVE mode and is asleep.
b) Check power to computer and LCD.
c) Check the cable connection from the LCD monitor to the computer.
d) Try a different monitor on the computer to isolate the problem to either the monitor or computer.
e) Remove power cords to monitor and computer. Re-insert both cords back and power on monitor first, then computer.

PRINTER DOESN'T PRINT

a) Restart the printer and computer.
b) Try a printer test directly from the printer.
c) Check the cartridge ink levels.
d) Try to print a Windows Test Page to determine if the problem is with Windows or an application program.
e) Uninstall and re-install the printer driver software.
f) Install the printer on a different computer to determine if the problem is with the printer or the computer.

NOTEBOOK WON'T POWER UP

a) Remove the notebook battery from the notebook and restart.
b) Try a replacement power supply.
c) Connect an LCD monitor to the notebook VGA port connection and restart the computer. If an image appears on the external monitor, the notebook has a LCD screen problem or inverter problem.
d) If the jack connection is loose or can be wiggled, the jack has to be soldered or replaced.

WINDOWS BLUE SCREEN ERROR MESSAGE

a) Does the message say anything about a bad hard drive or bad memory? If so test or replace either the memory or hard drive. Reseat the memory or replacing the memory in a different slot.
b) Power the computer off, disconnect all peripheral devices connected and restart the computer without any device connections. If the computer restarts, add a single device on each restart to determine which device is causing the problem.
c) Run in SAFE MODE. If the computer doesn't startup in Safe Mode, re-install Windows.
d) Check for and remove viruses.
e) Attempt to roll back the video driver or last device driver updated.
f) Download and run the Microsoft FIXIT program.

GENERAL TIPS

1. **Turn off and repower everything.**
2. **Attempt to undo the last thing done prior to the problem starting.**
3. **If the computer doesn't start in SAFE MODE, it needs a Windows Re-installation.**
4. **GOOGLE the problem.**

g) Glossary

www.ingramcontent.com/pod-product-compliance
Lightning Source LLC
Chambersburg PA
CBHW080357060326
40689CB00019B/4043